Android™ Auto Tour Guide
App Development for Android Auto

Android™ Auto Tour Guide

App Development for Android Auto

Sanjay M. Mishra

Printed by *CreateSpace*

First published :   April 2016

ISBN-13   :   978-1518672460
ISBN-10   :   1518672469
LCCN   :   2016904359

Table of Contents

Part I   IN-VEHICLE INFOTAINMENT & ANDROID AUTO

Chapter 1   General Background

Part II   DEVELOPMENT BASICS

Chapter 3   Development Environment Setup

Chapter 4   Hello Auto

Part IV   MESSAGING & AUDIO APIS

Chapter 7   Android Auto Messaging

Chapter 8   Android Auto Audio

Part V   THE ROAD AHEAD

Chapter 9   Future directions

Foreword
by Nathan Blair

With the introduction of the Android platform, Google forever changed the landscape of open, mobile, and ubiquitous computing; Android Auto continues that trend by seamlessly extending connectivity and interaction to automobiles, providing end users with an engaging and contextual driving and infotainment experience while simultaneously supplying developers with a delightful, flexible, and generally intuitive application creation experience.

Android Auto Tour Guide takes you on an exciting expedition through the Android Auto ecosystem with an approachable, yet thorough and timely overview. Everything you need to get started is covered here, from an overview of Android Auto to setting up your environment (including the hardware for your vehicle!) to building and debugging custom Apps that leverage the Audio and Communication APIs that work together to form Android Auto. Beginners and experts alike can benefit from Sanjay's keen understanding and clear composition. The rich code examples and copious diagrams and figures converge to provide the depth and context needed for a clear understanding of the material at hand, giving you the foundation you need to explore and realize your own ambitions for successful Auto Apps.

Sanjay pours his contagious enthusiasm and impressive expertise into each page, making this book entertaining as well as informative. I am proud to call him a coworker, co-conspirator, and most importantly, friend. It has been an exciting honor and privilege to peek behind the curtain and observe the evolution of his work, from the early stages of outlines and notes through the completion of this book that you are now holding.

I hope you will enjoy this book as much as I have. May it launch you down the road to success for all of your Android Auto ambitions. So sit back, fasten your seat belt, start your engine, crank up some music, and prepare for a fascinating ride through Android Auto with the *Android Auto Tour Guide*!

Nathan Blair
Denver, Colorado
March 2016

Foreword
by Rudi Cilibrasi

As a veteran computer programmer from the pre-Internet era, I have seen shifts and swells in the sea of technology time and again. If anything, I have learned that skills make the programmer, and one cannot ever learn enough to keep up with the explosive growth of technology around the world. It is necessary to grab onto one rung after another in the ladder of technology ever reaching higher to stay relevant, efficient, and modern. By now I have understood that it is only possible for me to learn a small section of this great wave of engineering that has transformed our way of life, and the pace has humbled me. This humility has led to an easy, laid-back style of learning through practice and casual conversation with friends to get pointers about the right areas to learn at the right times: I cannot hope to watch the fractal edge of technology as a whole, but I can continue to stay connected to the best and brightest colleagues who have impressed me the most as coworkers over the years in industry.

To ignore the mobile revolution is to ignore the bulk of modern personal computing and networking in the twenty-first century. I've strived to keep up with the basics of iOS, Android, and web hybrid mobile development by enjoying personal projects and occasional paid jobs over the last decade. Although my main focus has been on back-end server web development, I am no stranger to Android applications and want to continue to play in that arena. It has been my privilege to work with and dialogue with Sanjay Mishra, a passionate, committed, and comprehensive student and master of Android technology. I was surprised when I heard about Sanjay's new book on using Android in automobiles because I had not realized Android had already made that inroad so far and so quickly. Like his previous book *Wearable Android – Android Wear & Google Fit App Development*, this tome adopts an easygoing and personable tone that is both welcoming and detailed without sacrificing quality. Unlike most other technical books, this one does not surrender to inscrutability in any part and provides plenty of practical examples with diagrams and screen-shots to allow easy crystallization of the information for readers at any level of experience. The humility and confidence communicated in this practical volume makes the work involved in getting started in programming for Android Auto seem to shrink to insignificance. I invite you to jump in and give it a try. Why not take a relaxing ride along the Android highway and let Sanjay do the driving until you too are ready to take the wheel?

Rudi Cilibrasi, Computer scientist

About the Author

Sanjay Mahapatra Mishra began programming in C on various flavors of Unix, in the early 1990s and soon began appreciating the Linux operating system, GNU, and open source software as well as the Java® programming language. Over the years, he has developed diverse software systems spanning web applications and services, VoIP, messaging, telephony, NoSQL, analytics, mobile and embedded devices; and worked for companies such as Dealertrack Technologies (Cox Automotive), Western Digital Corporation, Intertrust Technologies Corporation, Eyecon Technologies, Callsource, nVoc (formerly Sandcherry, Inc), and Starz Entertainment Group.

Sanjay holds a Bachelor's Degree in Electrical Engineering from the University of Poona (Pune) in India and possesses five Sun Microsystems certifications since 1998 as Java Programmer, Java Developer, Java Platform Architect, Java Enterprise Architect and Java Web Services Developer. Sanjay is also the author of *Wearable Android : Android Wear & Google Fit App Development* published by John Wiley & Sons, Inc., and has a Google+ profile at: *https://plus.google.com/+SanjayMishra369*.

Nathan Blair

Nathan wrote his first program in BASIC on a TRS-80 under the guidance of his grandmother and quickly discovered that programming and computers were his passion. Since then, he earned a Bachelor of Science degree in Computer Science from New Mexico Institute of Mining and Technology and a Master of Engineering degree in Computer Science from the University of Colorado Boulder. He has worked in several industries, including energy, telecommunications, application performance management, utilities, and entertainment, and has experience in a wide variety of platforms and languages. Nathan currently lives with his family in Denver, Colorado.

Rudi Cilibrasi

Rudi is a full stack developer with interests in mathematical algorithms, scientific programming, and data compression. He has enjoyed working in the computer industry for decades in startup companies at every technical level. As an open source programmer and ongoing practitioner, he appreciates the opportunity to learn a new programming language or launch a new website with the help of friends. A craftsman of programming, he enjoys the social as well as technical aspects of the culture and cannot resist sharing his enthusiasm with others through participation in challenges, contests, lively discussions, and the machine learning community. Rudi holds a PhD in Computer Science specializing in Machine Learning from the University of Amsterdam and loves to apply the principles he learned there about machine learning to new applications.

Jahnavi Lokre

Jahnavi is a developer of innovative medical devices and clinical diagnostic systems both in startup and established companies. She is interested in machine learning and artificial intelligence applications related to life sciences. She also volunteers at local schools and organizations to promote STEM education among middle and high school students. She has a Bachelor in Electrical Engineering from University of Pune, a Masters of Computer Engineering from Texas A&M and a Masters of Business Administration from UCLA.

Acknowledgments

As a consumer and software engineer, it is delightful to have access to the multitude of computing devices and platforms that are available today, at affordable cost. The exploration of new and emerging computing devices and technologies in one's own personal computing laboratory is what makes this book possible.

I am particularly grateful to my dear friends Nathan Blair and Rudi Cilibrasi for writing their respective gracious forewords for this book, and also for their encouragement, insightful advice, and meticulous feedback — all of which were invaluable in improving the quality, content, and readability of this book.

I would also like to thank Jahnavi Lokre, Ajay Mishra, and Gene Amnuel for their valuable feedback on this manuscript. I would like to thank Scott Onstott for his general advice on the subject of self publishing. Over the years, I am grateful for the encouragement from my parents, siblings, classmates, co-workers and friends. I would like to thank Suresh Joshi, Manny Bhangui, Richard Steele, Jie Li, Bobbie A. McGee, Bobbie Pitzner, Uday Natra, Larry Muirhead, Martin Wills, Dawn Minix, Mike Gavaghan, Franz Zemen, Jeff Lutz, Nathan Blair, Jon Ford, Linda Gonzales, Chris Butler, Li Wang, Sateesh Bajikar, Anita Bowles, Robert Nevitt, Krishna Kuchimanchi, Samir Sinha, Rudi Cilibrasi, Amita Chobhe, Bijay Mishra, Jahnavi Lokre, Ajay Mishra, Moe Mohmoudian, and Nader Abdelsadek for their collaboration and friendship.

Most of all, I would like to thank you — my gentle readers — for your trust in giving my book a chance.

About this book

Preamble

Automobile dashboards have included digital audio systems and even navigation systems for decades. Such in-vehicle "infotainment" systems have evolved over the years and today, many include functionality based on Internet access and Internet search, which are features that have traditionally been available via desktops, laptops, and mobile hand-held (phone and tablet) devices. Such in-vehicle infotainment systems typically exhibit a variety of user interfaces and application behavior depending on the manufacturer and/or the model. Today, many in-vehicle infotainment systems lack a user experience that is user-centric and device-independent, and one that engages seamlessly with the rest of the consumer digital ecosystem of contacts, calendars, and music. In-vehicle infotainment is an important part of the overall ecosystem of automobile, transportation, and personal and cloud computing.

Android™[1] Auto

As consumers, most of us have likely experienced the inconvenience of having to deal with widely varying interfaces and behaviors in different automobiles' dashboards, as well as the overhead of having to setup one's contacts, preferences, and settings, when using an in-vehicle infotainment system the very first time. In such a backdrop, a platform such as *Android Auto* can extend the successful and popular **Android** mobile phone platform – that consumers are already intimately familiar with – into the automobile and its navigation, audio, and communication functions; thereby making a standard, in-automobile infotainment system both available to consumers, and equally importantly integrated with the rest of the consumer digital ecosystem comprising of calendars, contacts, and music. *Android Auto* is a collaborative effort and part of the ***Open Automobile Alliance*** whose members include over 38 major automobile makers, as well as several major audio player manufacturers and chip makers.

Many consumers end up driving more than one car model within a week, month or year -- due to reasons such as business or leisure travel, and/or the existence of multiple automobiles within the same household. *Android Auto* as a common platform across

---

1   Android is a trademark of Google, Inc.

automobile models can be relevant and convenient, as users will tend to appreciate an audio and navigation system experience that has a consistent and familiar set of interfaces and application behavior across automobile manufacturers and models. Users will also likely appreciate an experience that spans their mobile phones and in-vehicle infotainment system, while retaining their preferences, contacts, calendars, and their current context. *Android Auto* aims to serve as an in-vehicle extension of the Android experience that emphasizes hands-free voice and audio based interaction, while minimizing driving-unrelated visual content. *Android Auto* as a platform emphasizes safety as well as a rich user experience based on the convergence of the user's context across their phone and automobile. Since the invention of the motor car and the success of its mass manufacturing and mass consumer adoption, about a hundred years ago, the basic paradigm of the automobile had remained relatively unchanged for many decades, though the technology has certainly been evolving. Today, the ecosystem of the automobile transportation itself has been undergoing significant changes in recent years. The arena of the automobile and transportation represents a new frontier of the convergence of digital user experience, computing, transportation, and more.

This Book

This is primarily a technical book on the *Android Auto* platform.

What this book covers

This book covers the exciting new frontier of the convergence of in-vehicle infotainment with the rest of the consumer digital ecosystem of Android mobile phones and the cloud. It begins with general background on in-vehicle infotainment systems and relevant industry terminology and standards. It covers the *Android Auto* platform from the ground up and includes the hands-on steps of installation and setup of an Android development environment suitable for *Android Auto,* running the *Android Auto* desktop emulator, and writing, running, and debugging *Android Auto* apps. This book is based on and covers the latest version of the Android platform at the time of writing, namely Android version 6 (**Marshmallow**). The sample code is based on the *gradle* build tool and the *Android Studio 2.0* (Preview) Integrated Development Environment(IDE). It also covers the *Android Auto* experience on a real vehicle. This book concludes with a chapter on the current trends and possible future directions of consumer transportation and in-vehicle infotainment.

What this book does not cover

This book does **not** attempt to provide any comparative analysis of competing automobile infotainment platforms from outside of the Android and Google ecosystem, nor does it thoroughly enumerate all such competing platforms (this is by no means a reflection on the merits of such competing offerings). This book does **not** cover the base Android APIs other than the particular APIs that have relevance to extending apps to *Android Auto.*

How this book is structured

This book has nine chapters and is sectioned into five parts, as under:

Part I Introduction to in-vehicle infotainment & *Android Auto* – covers the general background and the industry standards and technologies that are pertinent to in-vehicle navigation and infotainment systems. It introduces the *Android Auto* platform, and it's capabilities and core functions related to navigation, phone, and audio playback.

Part II Development Basics – covers the setting up of an Android development environment suitable for *Android Auto* application development, including the *Android Auto* emulator as well as the hands on steps of writing, compiling, installing and debugging *Android Auto* apps. It also covers the real world in-vehicle *Android Auto* experience, including the process of installing an after-market *Android Auto* head-unit in your automobile.

Part III Design Standards – provides an overview of the design principles and standards, as well as the *Android Auto* application review and release process.

Part IV Messaging and Audio APIs – covers the messaging and audio related APIs pertinent to extending application functions to the *Android Auto* platform.

Part V The Road Ahead – examines the possible enhancements to the *Android Auto* platform and the product opportunities that are likely to become possible. It also provides insight into the ecosystem of automobiles and transportation to connect the dots of the trends across human, technological, legal, and socio-economic factors. It covers the synergistic effects of technological advancements such as collision avoidance systems, self-driving cars, in conjunction with the social trends of rising car sharing and declining automobile ownership all of which will tend to influence the in-vehicle user experience.

Target Audience

This book has been written for technology, business, and product folk alike. Android/Java developers and automotive technologists who are interested in understanding the *Android*

Auto ecosystem will likely find this book of interest. No prior experience with in-vehicle navigation and audio systems is necessary. However prior knowledge of Android and Java are virtually prerequisites especially for engaging with the hands on development and sample code associated with this book. Although only a small percentage of Android apps will have relevance for being extended to the initial version of *Android Auto,* understanding the basics of *Android Auto* will make it easier to evaluate the possibilities for meaningful engagement with the automobile and the associated business opportunities. Because both the road map of your application platform and the capabilities of *Android Auto* will tend to evolve over time, it will be useful to stay abreast of the latest on *Android Auto* to evaluate the possibilities for engagement periodically. New product, platform, and business opportunities may arise as *Android Auto* expands in its capabilities and features in the future.

Software Requirements

The *Android SDK* and *Java® SDK (JDK)* are available for all the major Operating System (OS) platforms. The sample code developed for this book is OS agnostic. The hands on steps, labs and sample code for this book (and for that matter this book in its entirety) was written on the **Ubuntu®** Linux platform. Ubuntu® is a Linux® distribution from Canonical Ltd, which is a U.K. based company that markets diverse products and services that are based on an open source model. As such, Linux and Mac® are excellent platforms for Android and *Android Auto* software development.

Hardware Requirements

The hardware devices associated with using this book include the following:
>   a **Development Computer**
>   an *Android Auto* **head-unit** in your car (optional)
>   an **Android 6 (Marshmallow) phone**.

Development Computer

For general Android software development, the Android developer site currently recommends a desktop or laptop with over 4 GB of RAM and a powerful processor: http://developer.android.com/sdk/index.html#Requirements. Particularly for the purpose of developing for *Android Auto*, a computer with at least **8 GB** of RAM is advisable and a functioning microphone and speaker are essential. The *Android Auto* emulator which runs on the development computer, emphasizes voice based input and audio based output, in order to emulate the in-vehicle, hands-free experience. I used a laptop from **System 76** with 16 GB of memory and an Intel® Core™ i7 processor, running Ubuntu Linux 15.10.

Android Auto head unit device (hardware)

The audio system interface that typically resides in the center of the automobile dashboard is referred to as the **head-unit** in the auto industry. If you happen to own a car that has an *Android Auto* compatible head-unit, that would be perfect. If you happen to be considering purchasing a car in the near future, you may choose a model that has *Android Auto* support in its dashboard infotainment system, per the car manufacturer and model details available at https://www.android.com/auto. Otherwise you may consider purchasing and fitting an after-market head unit that supports *Android Auto.* Several after-market head units are available at around US $500. The cost of installation can approximate US $500 including the cost of adapter and cabling accessories. The actual price will tend to vary by car model. The number of electronic controls related to audio, microphone, and telephone that are available on your steering wheel which will need to get hooked up with your after-market *head-unit* will tend to affect the labor effort – and ultimately the total installation cost. If you are considering purchase of an after-market unit, any in-vehicle/ in-dash navigation and entertainment system that clearly declares support for **Android Auto** should work out fine, at least in theory. Please be guided by the specification sheets and online reviews per your judgment, in order to choose a suitable *Android Auto* device.

This book uses an aftermarket *Android Auto* head unit, namely the **Pioneer AVIC-8100NEX In-Dash Navigation System®** for a real world exploration of *Android Auto* and it's in-vehicle driver experience. I purchased this unit on Amazon (amazon.com) at a price that was slightly less than US $900. The cost of installation of this head unit into the dashboard of my Toyota Camry Hybrid/2007 model was about $500. In the interest of safety, please seek the advice of your automobile manufacturer's authorized dealership with regard to installing an after-market in-vehicle infotainment system/head-unit. I did precisely that, and I strongly urge readers to do the same, as safety considerations are paramount. A physical *Android Auto* hardware based system – though ideal – is not essential for the purpose of learning software development for the *Android Auto* platform, as the Android SDK includes an **Android Auto head-unit emulator**.

Android Auto head-unit emulator (software)

The Android SDK provides an excellent software based **Android Auto head unit emulator** which runs on the development computer and gives you a good sense of the *Android Auto* user experience and provides a basic environment suitable for development, debugging and testing your *Android Auto* apps.

Android 6 (Marshmallow) Phone

Although *Android Auto* is compatible with mobile phones running Android version 5 (*Lollipop*) onwards, this book and its source code are targeted for Android version 6 (*Marshmallow*), the latest version of Android at the time of writing. This book endeavors to be future looking and therefore focuses on the latest core Android API.

Usage of terms

The term *automobile, vehicle* and *car* have been used interchangeably in this book. The terms *audio system, navigation system,* and *infotainment system* have been used interchangeably. The term *receiver* is yet another term that has been used for some time in the industry for the in-vehicle audio system, though its usage is on the decline and this book does not particularly use it.

The term *app* is a commonly used abbreviation for application, typically a software application. The term s*oftware application* and *app* have been used interchangeably.

The term *hand-held device* or simply *hand-held* refers to a phone or a tablet, which are devices that are typically held in the hand during usage. Because phones are more common than tablets, this book uses the term *phone* in many instances when *hand-held* might be more accurate.

The term **the** *Android Auto* **A**pp refers to Google's *Android Auto App* that is available on the Google *Play Store* at:
> *https://play.google.com/store/apps/details?id=com.google.android.projection.gearhead*.

There are many other Android **a**pps that have been (or will be) extended to the *Android Auto* platform – including Pandora, Google Maps, Google Music, as well as most significantly the apps that you might end up developing and releasing at some point; and these are referred to as *Android Auto* **a**pps. There is thus **one** *Android Auto App*, while there can be innumerable other *Android Auto* **a**pps – Android apps that have been extended to the *Android Auto platform* – any one of which may be referred to as **an** *Android Auto* **a**pp. This distinction will become clearer in subsequent chapters, and the terminology used aims to reduce potential confusion.

Conventions

The following are the typographical conventions used in this book:

Bold	is used to emphasize a word or term, and/or when introducing a new term.
Italic	is used to indicate literal terms such as product names, options on a device or application's screen, directory names, class and package names, and code snippets.
Italic Bold	is used whenever both the above criteria are met.
mono	is used to denote literal content such as commands that need to be typed – on the command line for instance.

Diagrams used in this Book

A few of the diagrams used in this book are from the *Public Domain*. Several diagrams used in this book are covered by the *Creative Commons License* and have been attributed to their original creators per the terms of the license. The rest of the diagrams used in this book have been created by the author.

API References

This book is based on the current Android platform API (Application Programming Interface) level at the time of writing – namely API level 23 (Marshmallow). It is expected that newer versions of APIs will get released that may have the effect of rendering outdated particular portions of this book's content. This is somewhat unavoidable and inherent to the nature of the publishing time lines in conjunction with the rapid evolution of mobile platform APIs.

Third Party, Online References

Third party online resources have been provided in good faith, but their content is not in the control of the author or the publisher. Links are subject to change without notice and may become defunct over time. Yet this book lists online resources due to their relevance at the time of writing. Neither the author nor publisher is responsible for the accuracy, relevance or suitability of third party online links and/or their content.

Book website

This book has a dedicated website: http://androidautobook.info with an index to all the online resources associated with this book.

Source Code

The entire source code associated with this book is available online and accessible via the above mentioned book website. Entire code listings have not been included in the contents of this book; the book uses nominal code snippets whenever relevant, in order to illustrate specifics points.

Errata

Any typographical errors, mistakes or ambiguity detected after publication will be listed and publicly accessible via the above mentioned website for the book.

Trademarks and Copyrights

Linux™ is the trademark owned by Linus Torvalds. Android is the trademark of Google, Inc. ARM® is the registered trademark of ARM Holdings plc. Ubuntu® is a Linux distribution and the registered trademark of Canonical Ltd. Java® is the registered trademark of Oracle and/or its affiliates. *Android Auto*, Google, ChromeOS, Chromebook, and *Google Play* are the trademarks, trade names or product names owned by Google, Inc. Mac, OS X, and CarPlay are trademarks of Apple Inc., registered in the U.S. and other countries. Intel® and Intel® Core™ are the trademarks of Intel Corporation in the United States and other countries. AppLink™ is the registered trademark of Ford Motor Company. All product and brand names referenced in this book are the property of their respective owners.

Driving and Automobile Safety Disclaimer

This book covers the topic of application development for Google's *Android Auto* platform. As an application developer and/or automobile driver, you are responsible for the safe upkeep and operation of your vehicle, and for your driving in compliance with your applicable local, state and national laws.

References

http://www.openautoalliance.net	Open Auto Alliance
https://www.android.com/auto	*Android Auto*, Android Inc.
http://en.wikipedia.org/wiki/Public_domain	Public Domain license information
http://creativecommons.org/licenses	Creative Commons License Information
http://androidautobook.info	This book's website for source code
http://www.canonical.com	Canonical Ltd.
http://gradle.org/	Gradle build tool

Part I   IN-VEHICLE INFOTAINMENT & ANDROID AUTO

This section covers the general background and the industry standards, technologies, and terminologies that are pertinent to in-vehicle navigation and infotainment systems. It introduces the *Android Auto* platform and it's capabilities and core functions such as navigation, phone, messaging, and audio playback.

CHAPTER 1 General Background

Before we venture into the world of in-vehicle infotainment systems, let us look at the bigger picture of consumers and their devices in a world of a multitude of devices that consumers may own and/or interact with in their daily lives. This chapter covers the numerous technologies, standards and concepts relevant to the ecosystem of consumer devices and user to computer interactions including in-vehicle infotainment systems.

Consumer Ecosystem of computing devices, interactions

The consumer ecosystem of devices includes a multitude of devices such as smart phones, smart watches, home appliances and home automation devices, television and game consoles, automobile infotainment systems, fitness peripherals, self-serve kiosks, and beacons. Some devices may be more intimately associated with the consumer/user (eg. smart watch, mobile phone), while others may be shared with others within a household and still other devices interact with the consumer and/or the consumer's intimate devices, on a more casual, ad hoc basis – for instance beacons at public or retail locations. Beacons are small battery powered devices that are typically mounted on walls or posts at bus stops, airports, and retail stores, and connectible via consumer's phones over Bluetooth Low Energy, in order to provide consumers with guidance and relevant location and contextual information. A beacon at a bus stop for example can help commuters with live information about bus schedules, routes and current status. Beacons can also be useful in office, home, and industrial environments for proximity detection and automation.

The Internet of Things (IoT) refers to the interconnected ecosystem of consumer electronics, household appliances, automobiles, health, medical, industrial, agricultural and public infrastructure "things" that have embedded computing devices and sensors with network connectivity. Users engage with these diverse consumer computing and IoT devices via various corresponding flavors of user-computing device interactions. The interaction is a function of the device form factor which represents the size, shape, layout, and capabilities of a consumer computing device. A good user to computer interaction also needs to take the user's current real world context into consideration. A smart watch based user interaction for example, needs to emphasize glanceable interactions that take up the user's attention for no more than a few seconds. A user who is currently comfortably situated and has access to a phone, tablet or netbook, is unlikely to use the smartwatch at that time to engage with the online, digital world. When the same user is out on an evening walk or run, the smart watch serves as the main medium of interaction with the digital world and the smartwatch based user to computer interaction therefore ideally needs to be glanceable (ie. requiring minimal attention, a brief glance).

Smart phone at the center

In such an ecosystem of a multitude of devices that a given user owns and/or interacts with, the smart phone has a unique place due to factors including its familiarity, portability, touch screen based interactivity, and ease of connectivity over various networking protocols and standards. Some IoT devices such as fitness sensors and home automation devices may have their own user interfaces while others do not as these are expected to be used via wired and wireless communication mechanisms.

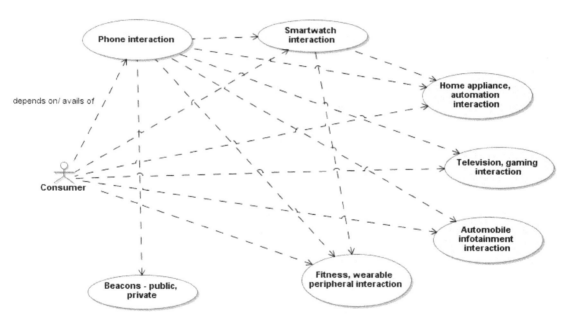

Figure 1-1 Consumer - Computing device interactions in a multi device world

While consumers may engage directly with the user interfaces of their various devices if available, the phone has a special place in the consumer ecosystem as it typically ends up serving as a central hub via which many interactions are channeled. Users find it convenient to simply connect their smart phone (over various connectivity technologies) to their numerous other consumer devices and interact via their smart phone based application user interfaces, even in case of the devices that have their own native user interface. As a hand-held device, the phone enjoys proximity to the user, and also has a certain minimal threshold of computational power, networking capabilities, and screen size. Figure 1-1 shows the various flavors of user to computing device interactions via which a given user may engage with various types of devices; it also depicts the engagement of the phone with other devices on behalf of the user.

Pervasive Computing

Pervasive computing – also known as ubiquitous computing – pertains to the availability of computing resources everywhere and all the time, via a multitude of network connected devices. The availability of mass market mobile phones and tablets, wearable devices, connected home appliances, and in vehicle infotainment systems has made pervasive computing a practical reality.

User Context

The user context pertains to what the user is engaged in, moment to moment in the real world – such as on a morning run, at dinner with family, driving to keep an appointment, on a vacation, and so on. The user-centric user context in such a pervasive computing environment spans the various personal devices that the user interacts with. This supports a seamless user experience that continues from when it left off as the user switches between different personal computing devices. For example, if a song is playing on your automobile's in-vehicle infotainment system when you reach your driving destination, you may wish to continue to hear the rest of the song via your phone and earphones as you leave your car and begin walking. Any system that makes it easy to do this is aligned with a user centric and device independent model of interaction.

Personalization

Personalization pertains to tailoring of content and services according to the individual user's interests and choices which may be determined based on machine learning and inferences (implicitly), or user settings (explicitly).

Recommendations and Suggestions

Recommendations and suggestions are an important aspect of the user experience and are aligned with the new "suggest" model of user to computer interaction. (In the "demand" model which has been the long standing and predominant model of user to computer interaction for a long time, users initiate the interaction by demanding information from their computing device.) In the "suggest" model, the computing platform also takes some initiative to present timely recommendations and suggestions to the user. Analytics, machine learning, and predictions lie at the heart of the suggest model. As computing infrastructure improves, computing systems are able to make higher quality timely and relevant recommendations and suggestions to the users.

User Agent

A user agent is a software application that is typically an endpoint of network communication. A user agent represents the user and acts on the user's behalf to carry out user actions and receive notifications and information updates. Examples of user agents include browsers, email clients, phone dialers, and perhaps self service kiosks. A smart watch or an in-vehicle navigation system may be considered to be a user agent as they are endpoints of network communication that allow the user to take actions, initiate communications and receive information.

Vehicle Telematics

Telematics is a broad category of technology that encompasses telecommunications, instrumentation and sensors, transportation and safety, as well as multimedia and Internet. Vehicle telematics pertains to the subset arena of vehicular technologies including in-vehicle infotainment. Vehicle telematics encompasses vehicular and road safety, communications and sensors, GPS, maps and navigation, and Internet connectivity. Telematics has many practical applications including vehicle tracking, fleet management, car sharing, and automobile insurance applications.

Automobile dashboard

The dashboard is the control panel in front of the driver which houses the vehicle's controls and instrumentation. The dashboard – or simply dash – includes the steering wheel, lighting and wiper controls, emergency flashing light control, and the cluster of primary instrumentation such as speedometer, tachometer, fuel gauge, gear and brake status, warning/malfunction lights for fuel, oil, and tire pressure. Secondary items on the dashboard include heating and ventilation controls, and air vents. Dashboards typically include their in-vehicle infotainment system or head-unit with one of more of the following features and functionality: radio, audio players, navigation systems and cell phone integration.

The information that pertains to the immediate needs of driving are displayed in the main instrument cluster (of the speedometer, tachometer, odometer, fuel gauge, gear status, engine malfunction lights).

Steering wheel, controls

The automobile steering wheel is a input device that primarily provides steering/directional control and the horn. In recent years, however the steering wheel has included several secondary convenience controls such as audio volume and music playback control, voice commands and mute, and phone controls, many of which integrate with the in-vehicle infotainment system and its functions.

Figure 1-2 Automobile steering wheel controls – audio, phone, microphone

Such steering wheel controls are aimed at driver convenience and safety; they make it easier for drivers to access various secondary functions while keeping their hands engaged with the steering wheel and the primary function of automobile steering control. Figure 1-2 shows the steering wheel in my car, which happens to include various controls associated with audio, phone and voice.

In-vehicle infotainment systems

Automobile dashboards have included a diversity of radio receivers, audio cassette and CD players, and even navigation systems for decades. In recent years, in-vehicle systems have commenced to offer touch screens as well as light-weight applications and menus – much like mobile phones and tablets. Such in-vehicle infotainment systems have begun to routinely include Internet access and Internet search – features which have traditionally been available to users via desktops, laptops and mobile phones and tablet devices. Additionally in-vehicle infotainment systems also come equipped with connectivity over Bluetooth, Wi-Fi and Wi-Fi Direct for interconnecting with the driver's and passenger's computing devices. Some systems connect to the Internet via the user's cell phone while others via separate cellular technology. The integration of the automobile user experience with the rest of the consumer ecosystem has much relevance today. The "connected car" has network connectivity, Internet access and provides integrated features such as maps, vehicle and engine metrics, music and driving, parking and roadside assistance. However what is possible to implement technologically will always need to be reviewed and tempered by safety considerations – which are paramount.

The modern automobile has over time, progressively, and incrementally increased its dependency on a variety of electronic and computing systems for its core functions. Although the infotainment system is a computing device, it is merely a very small sub-set of the computing infrastructure that resides in a modern vehicle. The infotainment system needs to be electrically isolated from the core vehicle computing system due to safety and security considerations.

In such a backdrop, the integration between the core computing system with the head-unit for the purpose of presenting and making available particular diagnostic, maintenance and status information has some relevance in the long term. Although from the perspective of engineering, the infotainment system represents the optional, non-essential system that complements driving, automobile drivers who depend on the infotainment system's maps and driving directions and enjoy the audio system, tend to place the infotainment system at the center of their consumer digital ecosystem. There is also a trend towards electronic systems such as backing and turning camera which are more effective and simultaneously have additional advantages over conventional mirrors – for example, better aerodynamics.

Head-unit

The head-unit is the term used in the auto industry to refer to the infotainment system that typically resides at the center of the automobile dashboard. The head-unit in a modern vehicle typically has a touch screen and is integrated with the microphone, audio system and phone system. Head-unit models have capabilities including maps and navigation, radio, audio and telephone integration over Bluetooth. Based on ergonomic and safety considerations, the head-unit is so located on the vehicle's dashboard as to be readily visible to – but not right in front of – the driver and comfortably reachable, while the driver's eyes are on the road. The head-unit is also referred to by terms such as "receiver" (from "radio receiver") and deck (from "cassette deck").

Proprietary in-vehicle infotainment platforms

OEM in-vehicle infotainment systems have typically exhibited – in recent years – a variety of user interfaces and application behavior that differs by manufacturer and even the model. Automobile manufacturers have now begun to recognize the relevance of a user centric and device independent user experience that transcends automobile makes and models and can engage third party app developers – as subsequent sections in this book will illustrate.

Automobile and infotainment technical standards, platforms

There is much precedent in the automobile industry for technical collaboration and the development of standards. In any industry, the existence of standards supports the design, manufacturing, quality, safety and interoperability of the technology and components. Particularly in the automobile industry, before an automobile can be sold in a particular country, it is required to be compliant with a multitude of regulatory standards and specifications pertinent to controls, crash-worthiness, lighting, emissions, pollution, and environmental matters, and more. Standards also make it easier – and sometimes even possible – for components from diverse manufacturers to integrate and inter-operate. In the ecosystem of in-vehicle infotainment systems, there are numerous industry standards bodies that develop standards for the automobile industry. There are several ISO standards for example, which address quality and interoperability making it easier for automakers and electronic suppliers to integrate the head unit with the vehicle's relevant electrical systems.

On the software side, there have been several open source based efforts at developing operating systems for in-vehicle infotainment systems. Many in-vehicle infotainment systems installed in vehicles run one of several such open source Linux flavors. Without consumers and automobile owners being particularly aware of it, most vehicles' head-units are powered by a port of a Unix-like(*nix) operating system. The most prominent of open source head-unit operating system endeavors is the one lead by the GENIVI Alliance.

This section provides an overview of some of the technologies, standards, and associated standards bodies that are have relevance in the auto industry as well the head-unit.

Society of Automotive Engineers (SAE)

The Society of Automotive Engineers (SAE) was founded in 1905, with the goal of developing technical and engineering standards via collaborative efforts between automobile manufacturers and parts suppliers. SAE is today an international body that publishes over 1600 standards and best practices for automobiles including engine characteristics, motor oil classifications, brakes, transmission fluid, on-board diagnostics and connectors, communication systems, electric vehicle charging systems, head lamps, performance, durability, and ergonomics. SAE J1939 for instance is a prominent SAE standard that is pertinent to the communication and diagnostics systems in vehicular sub-systems and components. The Controller Area Network (CAN) is a formal set of protocols pertinent to the internal communications and messaging between components within automobile (as well as bus, train, aircraft, ship, and industrial equipment). Local Interconnect Network (LIN) is a serial network protocol that addresses the communication between components in vehicles and can complement the CAN.

"Auto-grade" head-unit hardware chip-sets

The processors and electronic components that power head-units have unique requirements such as the ability to withstand wider temperature ranges and higher vibrations as compared to other consumer electronic items such as those that reside within the home or in hand-held devices for example. A large multitude of ARM based chip makers (including TI, STMicroelectronics, Freescale, Renesas, Qualcomm, Broadcom, and NVIDIA) as well as Intel (with its lower power consuming chip sets from the x86 family) offer automobile-grade chips and modules that have been stress tested and certified as "auto-grade". The availability of inexpensive hardware in a dynamic and competitive marketplace makes it possible for affordable infotainment systems to be more universally available in automobiles, all over the world.

Automotive Electronic Council (AEC)

The Automobile Electronic Council (AEC) is a standards body that develops various specifications and standards for auto-motive electronics including head-units. Its members include a multitude of major automakers and chip makers. AEC's specification standards include the AEC-Q100 and AEC-Q200 series which address numerous physical, electrostatic and endurance standards for in-vehicle electronic components.

ISO 7736 (head unit size)

The International Organization for Standardization (ISO) works with its over 160 members organizations from over 200 countries to define standards for engineering, science and technology. ISO 7736 pertains to standardization of the physical dimensions of the automobile head unit enclosures. ISO 7736 stipulates that head units come in two sizes of 180mm x 50mm or 180mm x 100 mm. The dimension of the depth is not standardized. Head unit manufactures generally build units whose dimensions conform to this standard.

ISO 10487 (connectors)

ISO 10487 defines the standards for connectors that interconnect the head-unit to the automobile's electrical and electronics systems such as power supply, audio speaker's volume controls, phone mute control, CD changer, the navigation system, vehicle speed, and more (Figure 1-3). This standard addresses the dimensions and physical attributes of the connectors, as well as electrical and electrostatic performance characteristics.

Attribution: By Petter73 (Own work Petter73) via Wikimedia Commons, licensed under Creative Commons 2.5 [CC BY-SA 2.5 (http://creativecommons.org/licenses/by-sa/2.5)]

Figure 1-3   Standard ISO 10487 connectors for head unit

Automotive Grade Linux

Automotive Grade Linux (AGL) is a collaborative initiative driven by the *Linux Foundation* and numerous automakers, chip makers and entertainment device makers to enable the powerful open source Linux operating system for the automobile head-unit. More details are available at https://www.automotivelinux.org/.

The *Linux Foundation* in turn, is a non profit association that advances the Linux operating system. Linus Torvalds, the creator of the Linux kernel and operating system, works at the Linux Foundation. The Linux Foundation has over 180 corporate members including companies such as Redhat, Google, Facebook, Cisco, Yahoo, Oracle, IBM, Hitachi, NEC, Samsung, HP, ARM, Qualcomm, Seagate, and Intel. Several of the Linux based initiatives covered in this section have support from the *Linux Foundation*.

MeeGo

MeeGo was an initiative aimed at making Linux available for a host of device form factors including notebooks, tablets, televisions, set-top boxes and in-vehicle infotainment systems. The project ended by getting canceled in 2011, in favor of another initiative Tizen that had an overlap of purpose but was wider in scope. More specifics about MeeGo can be found at: https://en.wikipedia.org/wiki/MeeGo.

Tizen

Tizen is an initiative and Linux based operating system that is targeted for a wide variety of device form factors including PCs, notebooks, smartwatches, phones, printers, home appliances and in-vehicle infotainment systems. Tizen members include prominent electronic manufactures, chip makers and network operators. Tizen is a successful and currently active initiative and numerous consumer devices and appliances powered by Tizen continue to make their way into the mass market. More details about Tizen can be found at https://www.tizen.org/.

GENIVI Alliance

The GENIVI Alliance is a non profit organization and a collaborative effort that aims towards broad adoption of an open source in-vehicle infotainment system and development platform. The GENEVI Alliance was founded in 2009 and has over 160 members today that include prominent automobile makers (such as BMW, GM, PSA Peugeot Citroën, Renault, Hyundai, and Nissan), semi-conductor makers (such as Analog Devices, ARM, Broadcom, Freescale, Qualcomm, Texas Instruments, and Intel), electronic device makers (such as Pioneer, Clarion, Delphi, Bosch, Magneti Marelli, Mitsubishi Electric, LG, TomTom, Garmin and Marman) and middleware and service providers (such as Wind River, Nielsen, and Accenture).

The GENIVI compliant operating system is based on Linux and defines standardized API interfaces that make it easier for automakers and their suppliers to integrate their hardware and software stacks and components. Several major vendors such as Canonical (the creator of Ubuntu Linux OS, which I used to write this book and its sample code), Mentor Graphics, Monta Vista and Wind River provide GENIVI standard compliant OS implementations. Like Automotive Grade Linux, the GENIVI Alliance is a part of the *Linux Foundation*.

QNX for Automotive

QNX is a commercial grade Unix-like, real time operating system developed by QNX Software Systems (now a subsidiary of Blackberry) and is generally believed to be the industry leading automotive head-unit OS. In addition to the automobile and in-vehicle infotainment flavors of their OS, QNX also develops OS and software solution offerings for other industry segments such as medical, industrial, networking and defense.

Android, Automotive

A few head-unit models available in the marketplace use an informal fork of the Android Open Source Project(AOSP) – the repository of the source code for the Android OS that is conducive to customization and forking. There is incidentally no co-relation between the use of an Android derived operating system in the head-unit and its compatibility with *Android Auto.* Typically when a head-unit product is compatible with *Android Auto* or any other standard, there is little need for it's manufacturer to specify what OS it is running under the covers. Users are typically concerned with the supported consumer standards, rather than the underlying OS. Incidentally, Android as a head-unit OS is a marginal OS in terms of number of installations. Android itself being based on Linux, often gets categorized as a Linux or Linux-like OS, making this statistic even more difficult to track. Parrot Systems for one, manufactures infotainment head-units – mostly for the after-market segment – that are powered by a flavor of the Android OS. Some of their newer head-units support *Android Auto* at least for the OEM segment. More information on Parrot Systems is available at: http://www.parrot.com/asteroid-range/usa/.

Automobile infotainment - consumer standards

There are several standards pertinent to integration between smartphones and the in-vehicle infotainment systems. Two such standards are MirrorLink – which is an open and non-proprietary standard, and *SmartDeviceLink*, which was originally developed by Ford as a proprietary product and subsequently released as an open source project for wider industry adoption.

MirrorLink

MirrorLink is a standard that addresses interoperability and integration between the smartphone and the in-vehicle entertainment system. *MirrorLink* facilitates the display of smartphone application user interfaces in the in-vehicle infotainment system screen, as well as the transmission of user input from the infotainment system and steering wheel buttons to the smartphone. *MirrorLink* leverages non-proprietary and standard technologies such as USB, Wi-Fi, Bluetooth, UPnP, Internet Protocol and Virtual Network Computing(VNC).

SmartDeviceLink

SmartDeviceLink is a technology that was originally developed by Ford for its Ford SYNC in-vehicle infortainment system and its AppLink™ product. Ford's AppLink is a branded product that serves to integrate the consumer mobile ecosystem with the in-vehicle user experience. Under the covers, AppLink is dependent on *SmartDeviceLink* technology. Ford originally developed *SmartDeviceLink* and subsequently released it to the open source community in 2013 for wider industry adoption as an open standard.

SmartDeviceLink is now hosted by GENIVI and has the potential for wide industry participation. *SmartDeviceLink*, as a GENIVI project today, aims to make it easier for application developers to integrate their mobile applications to the in-vehicle infotainment system, while ensuring an integrated and consistent look and feel across automakers and models. QNX has been reported to plan on supporting the *SmartDeviceLink* standard from GENIVI, in their automotive offerings. Toyota reportedly has plans to support *SmartDeviceLink* in their in-vehicle infotainment systems.

This chapter provided a high level overview of the numerous technologies, standards, and concepts relevant to the ecosystem of consumer devices including in-vehicle infotainment systems. Although these two ecosystems have evolved independently over the decades, there is much relevance today for their integration so that consumers can experience a seamless, user-centric, and device-independent interaction.

References and further reading

https://en.wikipedia.org/wiki/Internet_of_Things
https://en.wikipedia.org/wiki/Ubiquitous_computing
https://en.wikipedia.org/wiki/Bluetooth_low_energy
https://en.wikipedia.org/wiki/Beacon
https://en.wikipedia.org/wiki/User_agent
https://en.wikipedia.org/wiki/Personalization
https://en.wikipedia.org/wiki/In_car_entertainment
https://en.wikipedia.org/wiki/Connected_car
http://www.wired.com/2015/08/chrysler-harman-hit-class-action-complaint-jeep-hack/
http://blog.caranddriver.com/bmw-gets-serious-about-replacing-mirrors-with-cameras/

http://www.wired.com/2014/04/tesla-auto-alliance-mirrors/
http://www.usatoday.com/story/money/cars/2014/03/31/nhtsa-rear-view-cameras/7114531/
http://www.arm.com/
http://www.aecouncil.com/
https://en.wikipedia.org/wiki/Vehicle_regulation
https://en.wikipedia.org/wiki/Automotive_Electronics_Council
https://en.wikipedia.org/wiki/Steering_wheel
https://en.wikipedia.org/wiki/SAE_International
https://en.wikipedia.org/wiki/International_Organization_for_Standardization
https://en.wikipedia.org/wiki/ISO_7736
https://en.wikipedia.org/wiki/Connectors_for_car_audio
https://en.wikipedia.org/wiki/Connectors_for_car_audio#ISO_10487
https://www.tizen.org/
http://www.genivi.org/
https://en.wikipedia.org/wiki/GENIVI_Alliance
https://en.wikipedia.org/wiki/Linux_Foundation
https://en.wikipedia.org/wiki/Drive_by_wire
https://www.linkedin.com/in/linustorvalds
http://www.qnx.com/solutions/industries/automotive/
http://www.qnx.com/products/qnxcar/
http://www.openqnx.com/
http://www.linuxfoundation.org/about/members
http://linuxgizmos.com/automotive-linux-summit-agenda-announced/
https://en.wikipedia.org/wiki/Linux_Foundation#Automotive_Grade_Linux
http://linuxgizmos.com/linux-based-in-vehicle-infotainment-on-the-rise/
https://en.wikipedia.org/wiki/Parrot_SA
https://en.wikipedia.org/wiki/Virtual_Network_Computing
https://en.wikipedia.org/wiki/Universal_Plug_and_Play
https://en.wikipedia.org/wiki/Wi-Fi
https://en.wikipedia.org/wiki/Bluetooth
https://en.wikipedia.org/wiki/Internet_Protocol
https://en.wikipedia.org/wiki/USB
https://en.wikipedia.org/wiki/Telematics#Vehicle_telematics
https://en.wikipedia.org/wiki/Intelligent_transportation_system
https://www.qualcomm.com/products/snapdragon/automotive
http://www.intel.com/content/www/us/en/automotive/automotive-overview.html
http://www.autoguide.com/auto-news/2015/01/nvidia-unveils-advanced-digital-cockpid.html
http://www.nvidia.com/object/drive-automotive-technology.html
http://www.ti.com/lsds/ti/apps/automotive/applications.page
http://www.csr.com/products/137/sirfprimaii
https://source.android.com/

https://en.wikipedia.org/wiki/Android_(operating_system)#Open-source_community
https://en.wikipedia.org/wiki/Ford_Sync#AppLink
https://en.wikipedia.org/wiki/SmartDeviceLink
http://techcrunch.com/2016/01/04/toyota-qnx-and-others-adopt-fords-smartdevicelink-platform-for-connecting-mobile-apps-and-cars/
https://en.wikipedia.org/wiki/MirrorLink
http://www.wi-fi.org/discover-wi-fi/wi-fi-direct
https://en.wikipedia.org/wiki/Virtual_Network_Computing

CHAPTER 2 Android Auto, Overview

Although in-vehicle infotainment systems have been available for decades, the in-vehicle user experience has historically tended to be isolated from the rest of the consumer's personal computing ecosystem. The in-vehicle user experience has tended to be hardware device-centric, whereas a user-centric model that spans the user's various computing devices is more appropriate. In-vehicle systems have often been in recent years, silos that lack ease of connectivity to and engagement with the rest of the consumer digital ecosystem of cloud based, user-centric contacts, calendars, communication and music.

Also, in-vehicle infotainment systems have tended to exhibit a variety of widely varying user interfaces and application behavior that is specific to the automobile manufacturer and model. Many of us end up driving more than one automobile model during the week, month or year, due to reasons such as travel and/or the existence of more than one automobile model within the household. What can be said to be lacking in the current ecosystem of in-vehicle infotainment, is a user experience that spans the user's mobile phone, desktop and automobile, as applicable to the user's context and preferences, calendar, contacts, and music; and a user experience that spans different vehicles that a given user may end up driving. As drivers and consumers, many of us have likely experienced the inconvenience and even frustration of cumbersome steps for getting setup with and actually using an in-vehicle infotainment system for the first time.

In such a backdrop, a platform such as *Android Auto* has the ability to integrate the automobile experience with the rest of the consumer ecosystem – of calendars, contacts, communications, music and driving destinations. Users will tend to appreciate an unified and integrated experience across their phones, tablets, desktops and the in-vehicle infotainment system, that retains their current context, preferences, calendars and contacts and most of all has negligible overhead of using a vehicle's infotainment system the very first time.

Application developers too will tend to benefit from a unified platform on which apps can be written in a manner that is not specific to the automobile's head-unit manufacturer and/or model. Much as the standards for the head-unit's hardware electronic components and accessories boost portability and inter-interoperability and reduce costs for automobile and electronics hardware makers, the existence of a application software platform standard that spans automobile and electronic manufacturers and models reduces effort and costs for application developers.

Android Auto serves as an in-vehicle extension of the Android phone experience that emphasizes safety and hands-free, voice and audio based human-computer interactions, while minimizing driving-unrelated content. *Android Auto* integrates with the head unit and the steering wheel controls to give drivers an integrated automobile experience.

Google Maps and Google Play Music happen to be enabled for *Android Auto* as anyone might expect, along with several other popular consumer apps such as Pandora and Spotify. *Android Auto* is compatible with mobile phones running Android 5 / Lollipop and later versions. Voice input, touch screen, and hardware buttons on the head-unit serve as input mechanisms. Although the touch screen and hardware buttons are available to the driver, the hands-free, voice based commands interface is encouraged and emphasized.

Open Automotive Alliance

The *Open Automotive Alliance* which was announced in early 2014, is a global alliance of technology and automobile companies committed to extending the Android platform into automobiles. About 38 auto makers and 20 technology partners are part of the *Open Automotive Alliance*. The *Android Auto* platform is a part of the *Open Automotive Alliance*. The list of companies who are expected to (or already) support *Android Auto* include Abarth, Acura, Alfa Romeo, Audi, Bentley, Chevrolet, Chrysler, Dodge, Fiat, Honda, Hyundai, Infiniti, Jeep, Kia, Maserati, Mazda, Mitsubishi, Nissan, Opel, RAM, Renault, SEAT, Skoda, Subaru, Suzuki, Volkswagen, Volvo, as well as audio system makers and technology partners including JVC Kenwood, Pioneer, Panasonic, Clarion, LG, NVIDIA, and CloudCar.

Hyundai became the first auto manufacturer to offer *Android Auto* (in its Sonata model) in May 2015, followed by Honda (Accord model) and Skoda (Fabia, Superb, and Octavia models). Pioneer offers three after market head-unit models at the time of writing, including the one that I procured and utilized in the writing of this book.

Many automobile manufacturer members of the *Open Automotive Alliance* are also a part of the GENEVI Alliance. The goals of these two organizations may be more complementary rather than competing. That's because *Android Auto* is – at least for now – not a flavor of the Android operating system (OS) targeted for in-vehicle infotainment systems like for example, *Android Wear* or *Android TV*, which are each specialized versions of the Android

OS. Many head-units that run GENIVI's infotainment system OS support the *Android Auto* platform. Even if the *Open Automotive Alliance* were to develop a head-unit OS in the long run, that would represent a continuation of the basic principle of collaboration across manufacturers, in the interest of greater portability and standardization.

Android Auto projection standard

Android Auto is a smartphone extension or projection standard that enables mobile devices running the Android OS to be operated via the in-vehicle dashboard infotainment system/head-unit. The head-unit serves as an external display for the Android mobile phone device and specifically the *Android Auto* App that's available on the Google Play Store and bridges the phone to the head-unit. It runs the application logic and directs visual and audio output via the head-unit's display and audio system. Similarly the Android mobile device receives and processes touch and audio input via the head-unit's touch screen and microphone. The *Android Auto* platform requires that the vehicle has a head-unit that supports *Android Auto*, the driver's Android phone runs Android version 5 or newer, and the *Android Auto* App from the Google Play Store has been installed on the Android phone.

Android Auto Phone behavior

When connected to the automobile's head-unit via a USB cable, the Android phone's screen becomes dormant and unresponsive to touch, it merely displays the *Android* Auto logo.

Figure **2-1** *Android Auto* phone screen lock

Simultaneously, the head-unit's screen and microphone engage and serve as input devices for driver interaction with *Android Auto* platform. The phone has it's output re-routed to the head-unit's display and audio system and receives input via the microphone and head-unit display touch. The phone's battery is also charged over USB during this time. Currently a wired USB connection is the only available mode of connection between the driver's phone and the car's head-unit.

Boosting Driver Safety

Because the Android phone's screen becomes dormant and unresponsive to touch when connected to the head-unit, it boosts driver safety – the driver loses access to the phone experience and is restricted to the *Android Auto* experience which is dedicated exclusively to driving.

Figure 2-1 shows an Android phone's screen, when it is connected to an *Android Auto* compatible head-unit. The phone's screen ceases to respond to touch events in this mode in the interest of safety. The user no longer has the ability to access any of the numerous apps installed in their hand-held device.

Figure **2-2** Android Auto compatible head-unit, in *Auto* "mode"

Simultaneously, the head-unit switches from its native interface to the *Android Auto* interface (Figure 2-2). The driver can access features that pertain to driving, or are permissible from the context of driving.

The *Android Auto App*'s various features and functions are dependent on the user granting permissions such as Location, Phone, Contacts, SMS and Calendar. Android 6 introduced a new permissions model that provides the user with the ability to revoke or grant permissions from outside the app via the OS Settings, at any time (Figure 2-3).

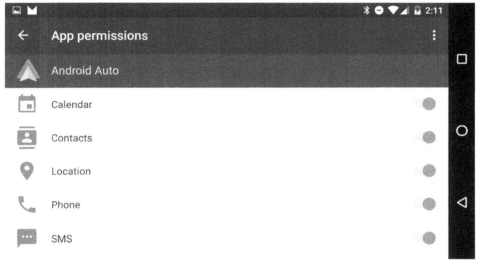

Figure **2-3** App permissions *Android Auto App*

Android permissions have undergone significant change in Android 6. Prior to Android 6, the consumer needed to accept all the permissions needed and requested by the application, as a prerequisite for installation of the application. The new permissions model represents a significant departure to the all-or-nothing paradigm of earlier. In the new Android 6 permissions model, users do not accept any permissions prior to application installation; they can do so when prompted by permission requests at runtime.

As an Android application developer, you will need to ensure that applications targeted to Android 6/API 23 check for permissions needed by particular application functions at runtime – every time – without attempting to store the permission status – as a shared preference or otherwise and request the user's permissions whenever a required permission is unavailable. Users can revoke permissions (or grant them) via the Android OS *Settings* – from outside the app – at any time. Your application will typically need to be designed to ensure that individual permissions that have not been granted by the user do not cause application crashes. The runtime permission checks in your application will typically need to be tied to the use case that requires the particular permission and simple explanations offered to the user as to why your application needs the permission.

Android Auto – **Vehicular data and resource access**

The *Android Auto* platform gains access to a wide range of vehicle resources including microphone input, speaker output, audio system as well as sensors such as GPS, compass, and speed. Therefore, the accuracy of directional orientation and current location are enhanced, which improves the overall maps and navigation experience. The table below enumerates the vehicle resources accessed by the *Android Auto* platform:

Vehicle resources	Available to *Android Auto*
Audio / Sound System	Yes
Microphones	Yes
Speaker	Yes
Steering wheel electronics controls	Yes
GPS antennas	Yes
Wheel Speed	Yes
Compass	Yes
Cameras	Future/anticipated
Car diagnostics, maintenance, fuel tank levels	Future/anticipated

In the long run, there is potential for *Android Auto* to access vehicle diagnostics, gasoline levels, mileage, engine and maintenance data and these can support many interesting and exciting use cases.

Android Auto applications

Android Auto applications execute, not in the *Android Auto* compatible head-unit, but on the Android phone that is connected to the *Android Auto* compatible head-unit over an USB connection. An Android-compatible head-unit is typically, itself a computer that runs a full fledged native OS(operating system).

When such an Android compatible head-unit is not connected to an Android phone, it is typically capable of running and displaying its own native applications and user interfaces pertinent to maps and navigation, music playback, telephony, settings and preferences and vehicle information, as applicable. When such a head-unit gets connected to an *Android Auto* compatible phone, it switches to *Android Auto* "mode" and relinquishes control of some its input/ output resources over to the *Android Auto* platform, which projects the *Android Auto* user experience. The head-unit serves as an accessory input-output device with respect to the Android phone.

The *Android Auto* platform also supports the extension of other *Android applications* into the head-unit. An *Android Auto application* is an Android application that has been extended to (or enabled) for *Android Auto*. Apps that are *Android Auto* enabled can extend their behavior into the *Android Auto* platform and the automobile's head-unit. Currently apps can extend their audio and messaging oriented functions into the *Android Auto* platform. In order for an application to be extended to Android Auto, it must target Android version 5 (API level 21) or later. This book and it's source code targets Android version 6 (Marshmallow), the latest version of Android at the time of writing.

The *Android Auto* platform is currently limited to serve as an extension-only platform, which means that writing an *Android Auto application* is necessarily about extending an Android app targeted to the Android hand-held platform, into the *Android Auto* platform. While an *Android Wear* application – for example – may have a binary/apk that can execute on an Android Wear device directly, there is at this time no such corresponding concept of an *Android Auto* binary apk that can actually execute on the *Android Auto* head-unit.

Android Auto protocol

The inter-working of the *Android Auto* compatible head-unit with the Android phone and the *Android Auto App* is facilitated under the covers by the *Android Auto protocol* library, which is available to *Open Automotive Alliance* members. The protocol library has binaries for Linux, QNX and Android head-unit operating systems.

The *Android Auto protocol* works over the USB connection and enables a bi-directional conduit that multiplexes and prioritizes the various channels of input, audio, display data, and sensor data (Figure 2-4), thus enabling the engagement between the mobile phone and the head-unit.

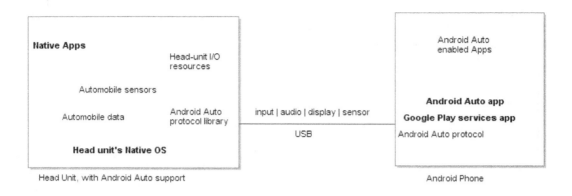

Figure **2-4** *Android Auto protocol*, head-unit, apps

While your phone is connected via the USB cable to your head-unit and the *Android Auto protocol* handshake is established, your phone and your automobile head-unit are engaged in *Android Auto mode*. A bi-directional channel gets established which allows the *Android Auto App* and the head-unit's I/O resources such as touch screen/display and microphone, to engage in the exchange of relevant data. Similarly sensor data – GPS, compass, and gyroscope signals and the wheel speed – available in the automobile become available to the *Android Auto* platform thus enhancing the accuracy of location detection and car's directional orientation. *Android Auto enabled apps* (or simply *Android Auto apps*) installed on the phone depend on the *Android Auto App* which acts as the gatekeeper for application interactions with the head-unit's display, touch screen events, and microphone input. Under the covers, Google's Play services app performs the deeper system level work needed for live *Android Auto* phone to head-unit interaction (besides a wide diversity of other functions such as location, maps, search, authentication, and support for *Android Wear* and *Google Fit*).

The *Android Auto protocol* itself is transport independent, so it is aligned with working over non-USB connectivity technologies in the future. Also, the protocol helps maintain OS independence, so that *Android Auto* compatible head-units may run various native operating system such as Linux, QNX, or Android. The *Android Auto protocol* in turn is built on top of the *Android Open Accessory* (AOA) protocol which allows USB hardware to interact with Android devices in accessory mode. More information on AOA can be found at: https://source.android.com/devices/accessories/protocol.html.

Advantages of *Android Auto*

The *Android Auto* platform offers advantages to consumers, application developers, automobile manufacturers, and head-unit/ electronics manufacturers alike.

Portability – across automobile and head-unit models

The *Android Auto* platform enables apps to work on automobiles from different automobile and electronics manufacturers, on a basis that resembles the write-once, run-anywhere model – app developers do not need to write separate applications for different automobile head-unit platforms. Given that automobile head-units have widely varying operating systems and hardware architectures such as ARM, MIPS, and x86 family chip-sets, writing independent head-unit based applications for the various niche head-unit operating systems and chip-set architectures can be complicated and even overwhelming for app developers. The widespread support that the *Android Auto* platform has from the auto industry is somewhat analogous to how the Android mobile phone OS created this vibrant and open ecosystem that helped mobile phone manufacturers leverage an open source phone OS and development platform that enabled app developers to write apps that worked across phone models, and underlying processor architectures – ARM, MIPS, and x86. The *Android Auto* platform thus takes care of the portability across the varying head-unit operating systems and processor architectures.

Also, a given user's phone may connect to different head-units at different times and a given head-unit may connect to different user's phones at different times, without any issues. Furthermore, there is very little overhead in the steps of connecting a particular head-unit to a particular phone for the very first time.

Ease of mobile app integration

The *Android Auto* platform enables Android phone apps to be extended to and integrated with the automobile head-unit with relative ease. Users typically keep their phones with them all day and for far longer than the time they may spend driving an automobile; the phone has access to the most current user context and data such as calendar, contacts, and relevant driving destinations.

Updatability

A mobile phone centric approach towards the in-vehicle user experience has the distinct advantage that the Android OS, the Google *Play Services app*, *Android Auto App,* and other *Android Auto app*s can be updated as frequently as necessary via the Google Play Store. If you have ever had to purchase a more current DVD with map and navigation data for your car, you will recognize the advantage of a phone centric in-vehicle driver experience. *Android Auto*'s phone centric approach thus keeps the *Android Auto* experience current and up to date – Google *Play Services app, Android Auto App*, and any app that has been extended to *Android Auto* (eg. Google Maps, Google Music, Pandora) can all be updated as needed, and per the consumer's preferences.

User centricity

The *Android Auto* experience is user centric and device agnostic. A given user with an Android phone can have an *Android auto* experience that is centered around their music, calendar, contacts, and driving destinations across their desktop, phone, smartwatches and automobile dashboard. Information such as destinations mapped, music played, calendars updated via the browser, smartphone, or smartwatch can be used for creating a relevant in-vehicle experience.

Co-existence with other in-vehicle infotainment systems

Support for *Android Auto* is intended to co-exist with the infotainment system's native operating system and the native non-Android maps, music, and telephony apps that are typically available from the automaker and/or the electronics maker. *Android Auto* also co-exists with the *Android Auto* compatible infotainment systems' support for competing infotainment platforms such as Apple's Carplay®, MirrorLink and so on.

Most of the auto-makers who support the *Android Auto* standard are also engaged in building alternate head-unit platforms. Making their automobile head-units *Android Auto* compatible means allowing the driver's Android phone to project the user experience to the head-unit while giving the user the choice to use the native in-vehicle infotainment system as well as other consumer standards and platforms.

Co-existence with other in-vehicle infotainment platforms and/or standards is obviously one of the reasons that most major auto-makers and electronics manufacturers are able to participant in the *Android Auto* platform and the *Open Automotive Alliance*, despite the fact that most participating auto-makers and electronics manufacturers have been and continue to be vested in one or more forms of alternate in-vehicle infotainment software platforms. *Android Auto* is thus an inclusive and co-existence friendly standard. The fact that the *Android Auto* platform currently limits itself to serving as a projection standard makes it easier for auto and audio system manufacturers to participate in it, while simultaneously offering alternate offerings.

Maximizing consumer choice

As the *Android Auto* platform can co-exist with the head-unit's native OS, suite of applications, and support for alternate standards such as MirrorLink and Apple's Carplay®, it has the effect of giving consumers the choice of their desired in-vehicle infotainment system and user experience.

Safety

Last but not the least, the *Android Auto* platform emphasizes driver safety across the mobile phone and the automobile head-unit and maintains application behavior that is consistent with various national automobile safety standards for head-units. While the phone is in *Android Auto mode*, it enforces the *Android Auto* screen lock such that the phone screen becomes dormant and the driver is constrained to engage exclusively via the *Android Auto* head-unit based interaction and driver experience, which excludes access to all functions that are inconsistent with driving – the driver cannot for example, use an Internet browser or watch a video or check their email.

Significance of *Android Auto* support in the automobile head-unit

Android as a mobile phone OS has the majority of the worldwide market share of phones, and many Android users are likely to value an Android experience that extends into their automobile dashboard. There are well over 1 billion Android phone users worldwide, though not all are automobile buyers. For Android phone users who are potential automobile buyers, the choice of the automobile purchase will tend to factor in support for *Android Auto*. Most of the major auto-makers have found it worthwhile to support the *Android Auto* platform. Conversely, for a major auto maker to decline to participate in the *Android Auto* platform can deprive consumers of the choice of their favorite infotainment system.

Effects of an auto maker's lack of Android Auto support

There are at the time of writing, perhaps only two or three major automobile manufacturers who have decided not to support *Android Auto* in their automobiles infotainment systems. Android users will tend to take into consideration, the matter of compatibility of their in-vehicle infotainment platform with their phone, when making a car purchase decision. Many years ago, car buyers did not think all that much about the in-vehicle infotainment system's inter-interoperability and compatibility with the rest of their digital ecosystem. Today, consumer are more likely to have expectations of compatibility and integration in this regard.

As an example, I have personally historically exhibited a certain brand loyalty towards

Toyota, and am currently driving my fourth Toyota purchase, over a span of two decades. Based on publicly available information including the *Open Automotive Alliance* and *Android Auto* websites, Toyota is not, at the time of writing, a part of the *Android Auto Alliance* and has not announced any plans to support *Android Auto*. I have been an Android user for over 7 years and on my next automobile purchase, I will certainly place a certain importance on the matter of support for *Android Auto* alongside the usual matters such as the automobile's overall engineering, reliability, performance, engine, seats, steering, and cost. If I were to make a car purchase today, I would be constrained to pass on Toyota and purchase instead – for the first time in my life – a vehicle that is not a Toyota. I may not make the best statistical sample point for this analysis, due to factors including my extreme fascination for both Android phones and the *Android Auto* platform. Yet, the automobile industry is known for its stiff competition and even if a mere 3% of current Android users who are considering purchase of a car happen to place some emphasis on compatibility with *Android Auto*, lack of support for *Android Auto* (and other prominent, inclusive co-existence friendly standards) will likely result in loss of some sales for particular car manufacturers or models – whether obviously discernible or not.

This chapter provided an overview of the Android Auto platform and its place in the consumer ecosystem that includes the automobile infotainment system and the mobile phone.

References and further reading

http://www.openautoalliance.net
https://www.android.com/auto/
https://en.wikipedia.org/wiki/Android_Auto
https://mobiforge.com/news-comment/mobile-os-market-share-q2-2015
http://www.androidauthority.com/one-billion-android-phones-2014-583506/
http://www.theverge.com/2016/1/4/10702844/ford-motors-apple-carplay-android-auto-announced-ces-2016
http://www.nhtsa.gov/
http://developer.android.com/training/permissions/requesting.html
https://www.youtube.com/watch?v=KNKGM4ss5Sc

Part II   DEVELOPMENT BASICS

This section covers the setting up of a development environment for *Android Auto* and running the *Android Auto Desktop head-unit emulator (DHU)*. It progresses into the hands-on steps of writing, compiling, installing, and running our first *Android Auto* app. It also covers the real world in-vehicle *Android Auto* experience.

CHAPTER 3   Development Environment Setup

The software and hardware requirements for this book are listed in the *About this book* section at the very beginning of this book, under *Software Requirements* and *Hardware Requirements* (page xxvi). It is likely that you already have a functioning and current, basic Android development environment. For the sake of completeness though, this section covers the setup of the basic Android development environment from scratch, before proceeding into the specifics of setting up *Android Auto* development tools.

Android Development Environment Setup

The Android development environment comprises of the Java Software Development Kit (SDK) – also known as the Java Development Kit (JDK) – from Oracle, the Android SDK from Google, the Android Studio IDE and also the *gradle* build tool which you may install independently as I did.

The Android runtime which runs on the Android device, uses the now discontinued Harmony Java project from Apache Software foundation for the implementation of Java class libraries. At the time of writing, it has been widely reported that the next version of Android – Android "N" – will leverage OpenJDK rather than Apache Harmony for the Java class library implementation in the device's **runtime** environment.

OpenJDK is an open source implementation of the Java platform and a collaborative effort by Oracle, IBM, Apple and SAP. Since Java version 7, Oracle JDK has been based on the OpenJDK implementation. The Oracle JDK includes additional components such as WebStart which are not currently available in OpenJDK.) This change will pave the path for the use of the latest Java 8 features such as lambda expressions and aggregate operations in Android apps. Besides, there have also been recent developments in the Android compiler toolchain – such as *Jack* and *Jill*. *Jack* – Java Android Compiler Kit – is a new and currently experimental complier which converts java source code to the Android dex format directly, without the original approach of using a combination of tools such as *javac*, *jar*, *dx*, and proguard to accomplish this. Jack has its own .jack library file format for pre-compiled dex code allowing for faster compilation. *Jill* – Jack Intermediate Library Linker – translates existing jar library files into the jack format. More information on this topic can be found at:

http://tools.android.com/tech-docs/jackandjill.

Java SDK environment setup

The Java SDK includes both the development tools (such as *javac* the java compiler, and associated libraries and tools) and the Java Runtime Environment JRE (such as *java*, the Java Virtual Machine which enables the host computer to execute Java applications). When doing a fresh install, it can be useful to uninstall any pre-existing, undesired – due to version or vendor – Java platforms that may already be present on your system. You may find that you have a Java runtime (JRE) already installed on your development computer, however what we are needing is the full Java SDK (which includes a JRE).

Java SDK installation

The Java SDK is available at: http://www.oracle.com/technetwork/java/javase/overview/index.html. You will need to choose the appropriate binary depending on for your processor and OS – for example I chose *Linux* → *x86* → *64 bit,* to match my development machine's *64-bit Linux* OS. I opted for the tar/gz format and extracted the file into my */opt* directory. I renamed the top level directory to *jdk1.8*, eliminating the minor version information from the directory name, to keep the path simple, easy to remember and verify. I made a note of the installation location as */opt/jdk1.8* .

Gradle Installation

Gradle is available at http://gradle.org/. I downloaded the zip archive for gradle version 2.8 and unzipped it to directory: */opt/gradle* on my development computer.

Android SDK installation

The Android SDK is available at http://developer.android.com/sdk/installing/index.html. I chose to use the "*STAND-ALONE SDK TOOLS*" based installation, followed by the subsequent installation of the *Android Studio* IDE. You may prefer to use the "*ANDROID STUDIO*" based install rather than the "*STAND-ALONE SDK TOOLS*" based approach. I personally find it more effective to install the individual tools independently. It is advantageous to have a functioning command line environment in addition to the IDE environment. The command line environment has fewer variables, is generally more robust, and supportive of a pristine build. This approach helps in troubleshooting issues and also allows me to upgrade individual pieces of the stack in a modular manner.

As developers, we seldom can get by – at least in the long run – without getting involved with the underlying details. Particularly new additions to the core Android platform – such as *Android Auto* – may initially lack integration with the Android Studio IDE. The running of the *Android Auto* head-unit emulator requires – at the time of writing – certain steps to be executed via the command line. I have always found it useful and relevant to verify the core standalone tools independently, as a precursor to setting up the IDE environment. Particularly by getting setup with a command line environment, I was able to explore and use the Android Studio 2.0 (preview) more easily. I downloaded and installed the "STAND-ALONE" Android SDK tools under */opt/androidsdk.* I modified the name of the top level Android SDK installation directory to "*androidsdk*"-- as it is shorter and easier to remember and verify.

Verify your Android development environment

After installing Java SDK, Gradle and the Android SDK "STAND-ALONE" tools , I added entries into my *.profile* as under:

```
export JAVA_HOME=/opt/jdk1.8
export ANDROID_HOME=/opt/androidsdk
export GRADLE_HOME=/opt/gradle
export PATH=$JAVA_HOME/bin:$GRADLE_HOME/bin:$ANDROID_HOME/tools:
$ANDROID_HOME/platform-tools:$ANDROID_HOME/23.0.2:$PATH
```

After introducing the various tools in the *PATH*, the *java, gradle* and *android* commands should become resolvable. Figure 3-1A shows the use of the *which* command on Linux, for this purpose.

```
~ $ which java
/opt/jdk1.8/bin/java
~ $ which gradle
/opt/gradle/bin/gradle
~ $ which android
/opt/androidsdk/tools/android
~ $
```

Figure 3-1A verifying environment using *which* command

I was also able to verify that the expected versions of the android tools were engaged via my command line terminal (Figure 3-1B). Next, I ran the *android* command to start the Android SDK Manager(Figure 3-2A). You will find that a few packages are already selected by default. Recent versions of *Tools*, recent API levels and all the *Extras* make a good set for additional selection.

```
~ $ java -version
java version "1.8.0_40"
Java(TM) SE Runtime Environment (build 1.8.0_40-b26)
Java HotSpot(TM) 64-Bit Server VM (build 25.40-b25, mixed mode)
~ $ gradle -version

------------------------------------------------------------

Gradle 2.8
------------------------------------------------------------

Build time:   2015-10-20 03:46:36 UTC
Build number: none
Revision:     b463d7980c40d44c4657dc80025275b84a29e31f

Groovy:       2.4.4
Ant:          Apache Ant(TM) version 1.9.3 compiled on December 23 2013
JVM:          1.8.0_40 (Oracle Corporation 25.40-b25)
OS:           Linux 3.19.0-18-generic amd64
```

Figure **3-1B** verifying java, gradle versions

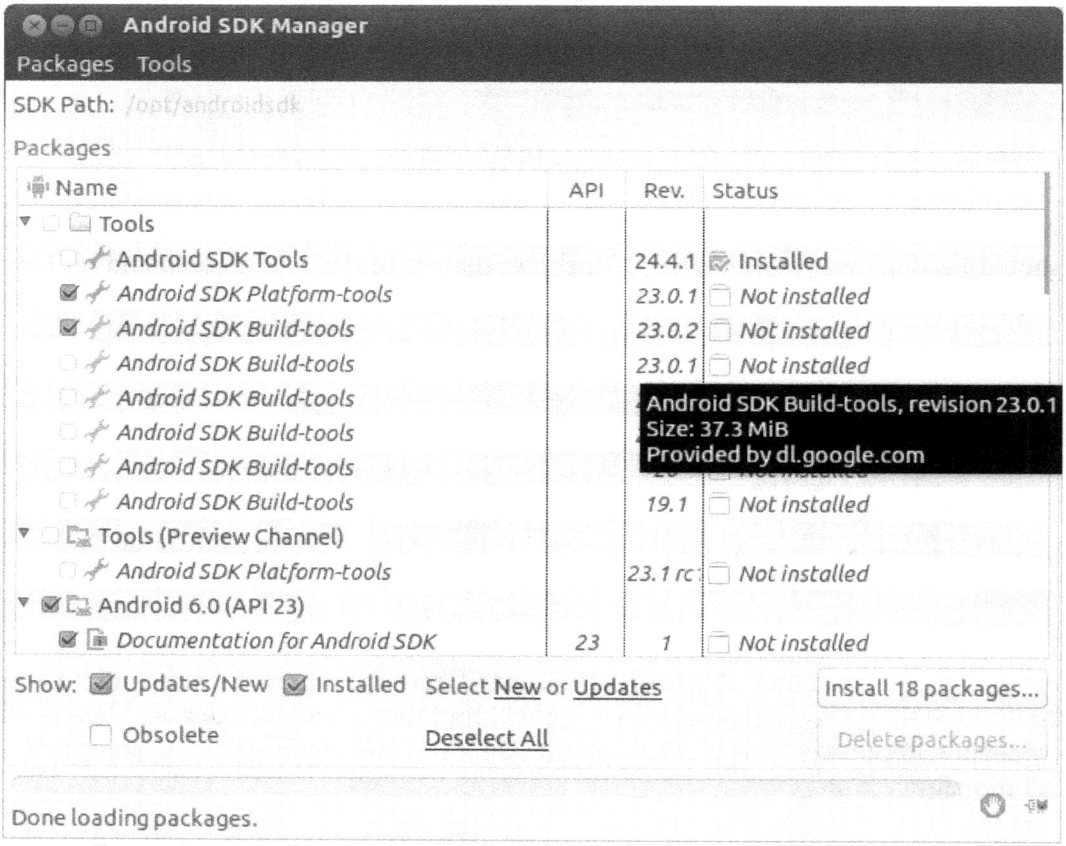

Figure **3-2A** Android SDK Manager, initial state, default selections

The actual number of packages will vary depending on the items you select. If you have a slow Internet connection, you may limit your selections to the most recent *Tools/* API levels and particular *Extras* : **Android Support Library**, **Android Auto Desktop Head Unit emulator** and **Google Play Services** library so as to have the most essential *Extras* readily available. Figure 3-2A shows the default package selections in the Android SDK Manager upon starting the **Android SDK Manager** right after extracting the binary, on Linux.

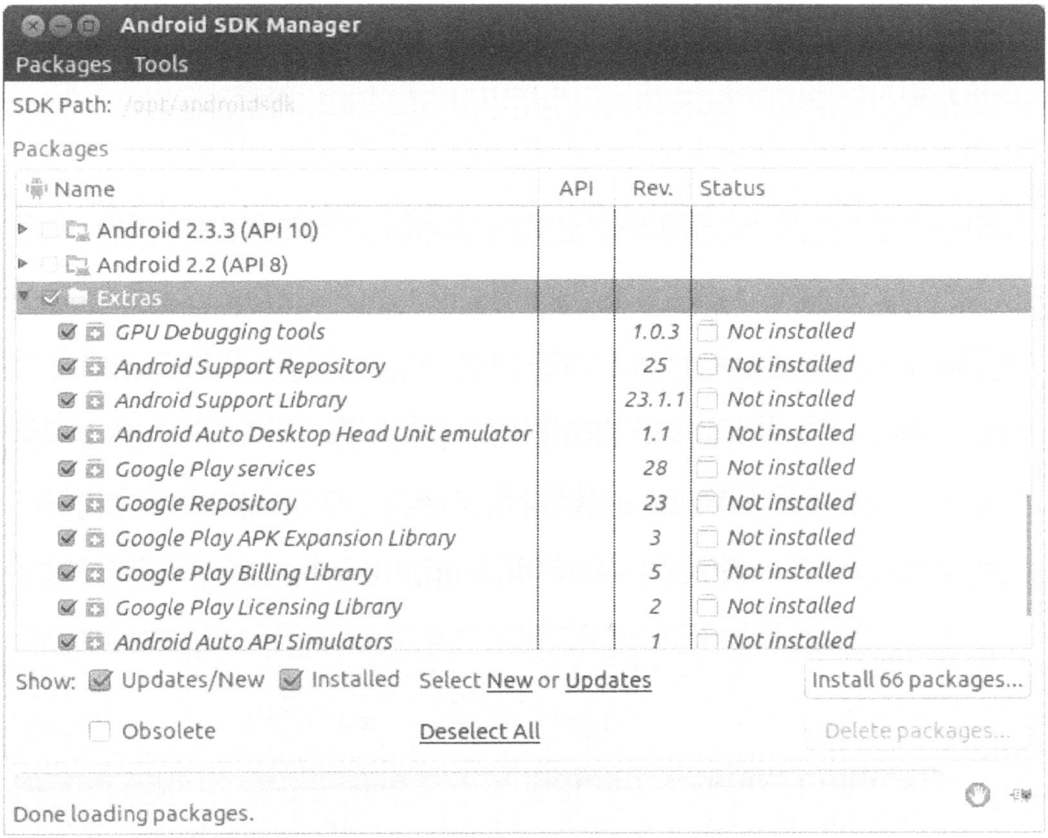

Figure **3-2 B** Android SDK Manager, with selections

Figure 3-2B shows my selection of 66 packages before I proceeded with the installation of the Android SDK packages. *Extras* also includes a GPU Profiler which depends on the recently introduced – at the time of writing – *Extra* : *GPU Debugging tools*. After the Android SDK Manager's installation process was completed (and that can take some time, depending on the speed of your Internet connection and the set of packages you have chosen), I compiled a random Android project from the Android SDK samples – to verify that the Android SDK is functional. I accessed the directory *samples/android-23/ui/views/CardView* under the Android installation directory via the command line and executed: *$ gradle installDebug* (Figure 3-2C). The build was successful and the built app executed fine on my Android device (figure not shown).

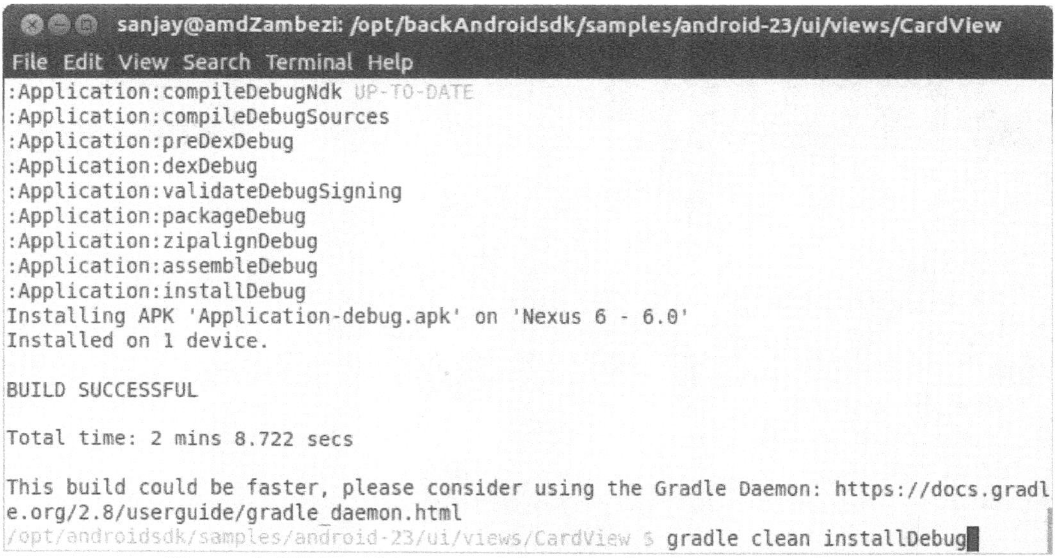

```
sanjay@amdZambezi: /opt/backAndroidsdk/samples/android-23/ui/views/CardView
File Edit View Search Terminal Help
:Application:compileDebugNdk UP-TO-DATE
:Application:compileDebugSources
:Application:preDexDebug
:Application:dexDebug
:Application:validateDebugSigning
:Application:packageDebug
:Application:zipalignDebug
:Application:assembleDebug
:Application:installDebug
Installing APK 'Application-debug.apk' on 'Nexus 6 - 6.0'
Installed on 1 device.

BUILD SUCCESSFUL

Total time: 2 mins 8.722 secs

This build could be faster, please consider using the Gradle Daemon: https://docs.gradl
e.org/2.8/userguide/gradle_daemon.html
/opt/androidsdk/samples/android-23/ui/views/CardView $ gradle clean installDebug
```

Figure **3-2C** Verifying standalone Android SDK installation

Once I had the base stand-alone Android SDK setup and verified, I was ready for the next step, namely the installation of Android Studio 2.0 (preview).

Android Studio 2.0 Installation

Android Studio 2.0 offers many useful features, productivity improvements, and performance improvements, several of which are described in this section. For more information on Android Studio 2.0 see http://tools.android.com/download/studio/builds/2-0-preview. I used the latest build of Android Studio 2.0 preview zip format for Linux at http://tools.android.com/download/studio/canary. I unzipped the file to a suitable location and then edited the file *studio64.vmoptions* in the *bin* directory under the installation home directory. I reviewed the heap sizes and ended up increasing the starting and maximum heap sizes (*-Xms256m* → *-Xms1024m*, and *-Xmx1280m* → *-Xmx1536m*), in order to better engage my development computer's available (16 GB) RAM. Figure 3-3A shows the first screen upon running Android Studio 2.0(Preview). I chose not to import settings from prior versions.

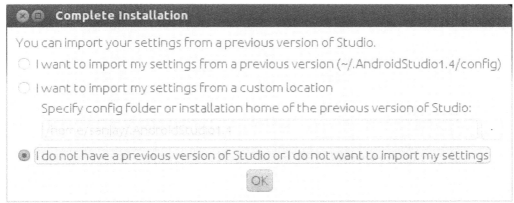

Figure **3-3A** Android Studio, first run, Settings import options

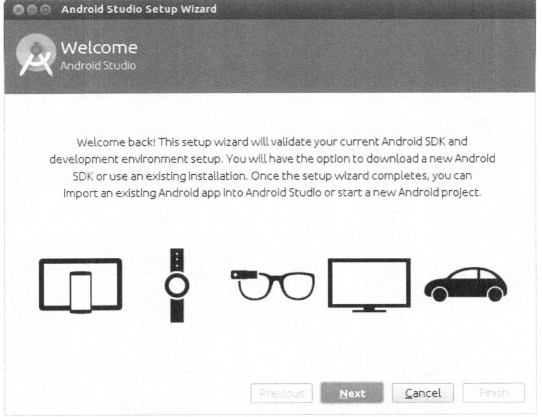

Figure **3-3B** Android Studio, first run, welcome screen

Figure 3-3B shows the *Welcome* screen, that includes the various device categories and form-factors relates to hand-held devices, wearables, television, and the automobile.

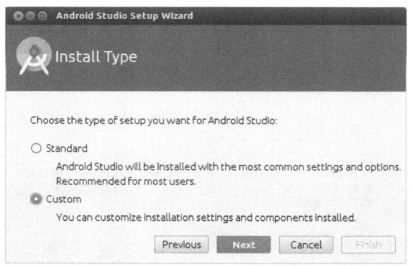

Figure **3-3C** : Android Studio, first run, Install type

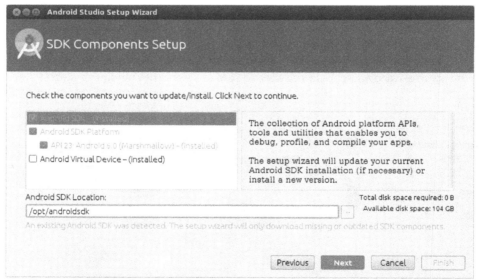

Figure **3-3D** Android Studio, first run, Android SDK location detected

Figure 3-3C and Figure 3-3D show the *Install type* screen and Android SDK location screens – I used the Custom option, so as to have greater visibility into and control over the underlying details.

Figure **3-3E** Android Studio, first run, Verify Settings

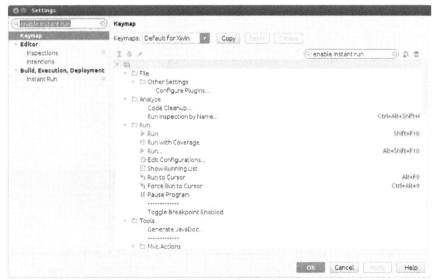

Figure **3-4A** Enabling *Instant Run*, for an Android App

Once I had Android Studio 2.0 installed, I imported an Android SDK sample project and was able to compile and run it via the IDE, both on a physical Android device as well as an Android Virtual Device (not shown in screenshots though, as it is quite straightforward).

To verify my Android Studio 2.0 environment, I wrote a simple *HelloStudio2* App and also enabled the **Instant Run** feature, that's new in Android Studio 2.0 (Figure 3-4A). *Instant Run*, as the name suggests speeds up the compile – install – run cycles after application code edits, thus improving developer productivity. More information of the Instant Run feature can be found at http://tools.android.com/tech-docs/instant-run.

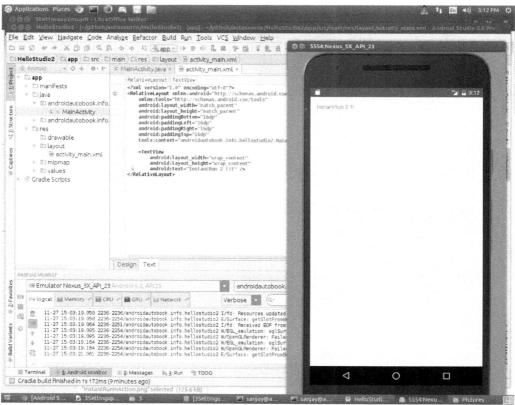

Figure **3-4B** Instant Run in action, instantaneous install-run cycles

After enabling *Instant Run*, the first time I installed and ran the app on an Android Virtual Device (AVD), it took the usual, perceptible duration of time to install and run. On subsequent install-run cycles – after layout and/or code changes – the changes rendered almost immediately on the AVD (Figure 3-4B). *Instant Run* works just as well, with a physical Android development device.

Fundamentally, Android Studio depends on the Java SDK and Android stand-alone SDK under the covers, in order to function. Android Studio is a top class IDE that provides many conveniences such as code formating, code completion, and UI design editors, while the Java SDK and Android SDK stand-alone tools perform the heavy lifting of compiling and building an Android apk. Android Studio (1.0) was first released late in 2015 and it has been rapidly improving in terms of new features and better integration with the underlying core tools.

Android Auto Head Unit Emulator installation

After I was getting the base Android development environment setup for the command line terminal as well as for Android Studio 2.0 IDE, I was ready to proceed into the world of *Android Auto*. Specifically on Linux based development computers, the *Android Auto* emulator requires several libraries, namely *sdl2, sdl2-ttf, portaudio*, and *png* to be installed. (Other operating systems do not have any such corresponding need.) On *Ubuntu* and other *Debian* based Linux flavors, the installation of these required libraries can be accomplished by issuing the following command :

```
$ sudo apt-get install libsdl2-2.0-0 libsdl2-ttf-2.0-0 libportaudio2 libpng12-0
```

The *Android Auto Head Unit Emulator* is available as one of the *Extras* in the *Android SDK*. You will need to ensure that this emulator has been installed in your development environment. Especially if you did not perform the steps of the fresh install earlier, you will need to start the *Android SDK Manager* by typing *android* on the command line, or via *Android Studio Tools → Android → SDK Manager.* (The visual elements and flow in the IDE may undergo changes over time while the step for running a command tends to remain unchanged.) Towards the bottom of the list of installed *Packages* under *Extras* (Figure 3-5A), you should see an item *Android Auto Desktop Head Unit emulator* along with its installation status. In case you happen to find that your *Android Auto* emulator shows a status of *Not Installed*, you will need to check the item and proceed to install it after accepting the applicable license terms. Most Android developers are already quite familiar with the various *Android Virtual Device*(AVD) emulators for the phone, tablet, Android Wear, and Android TV form factors. The *Android Auto head-unit emulator* that's available as part of the Android SDK serves a generally similar function, as a software based virtual device. However, you do not find it listed under the AVDs, as *Android Auto* is not a form-factor targeted flavor of Android operating system, as is the case for Android Wear and Android TV. After successful installation, *Android Auto* emulator binary which is named *desktop-head-unit* will be found under:
      <ANDROID_SDK_LOCATION>/extras/google/auto/ (Figure3-5B).

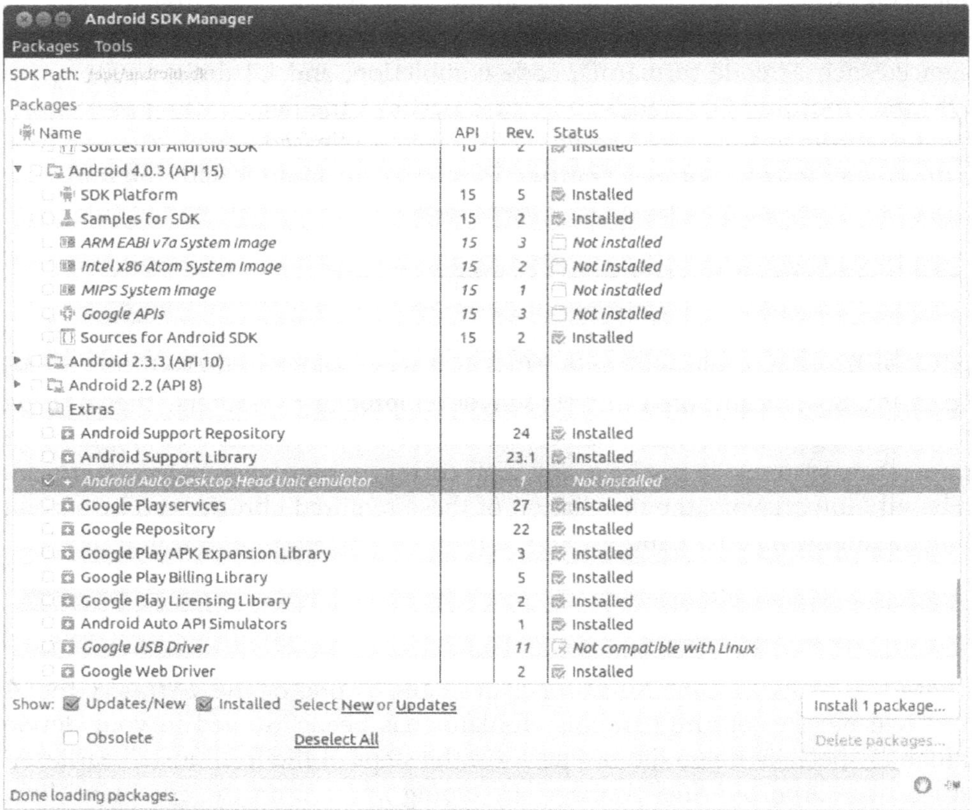

Figure **3-5A** Android SDK Manager /Extras/ *Android Auto* Emulator/ Installed status

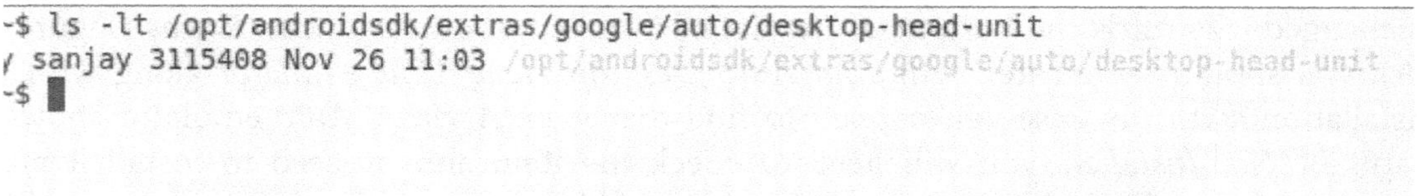

```
-$ ls -lt /opt/androidsdk/extras/google/auto/desktop-head-unit
/ sanjay 3115408 Nov 26 11:03 /opt/androidsdk/extras/google/auto/desktop-head-unit
-$
```

Figure **3-5B** Verifying the *Android Auto* emulator/ Desktop Head Unit (DHU)

I added *export PATH=$PATH:/opt/androidsdk/extras/google/auto/* into my *.profile* for consistent access of the *desktop-head-unit* program from my command line terminal. You may have noticed that there is an item under *Extras*, named "*Android Auto API Simulators*". *Android Auto API Simulators* which was released in 2014, has been deprecated; it was superseded by the more sophisticated *Android Auto Desktop Head Unit emulator*, released in 2015. Once you have the *Android Auto head-unit emulator* (also referred to as the *Desktop Head Unit* or DHU for short), you are ready to proceed to the next steps.

Android Auto app, Google Play Store

The *Android Auto* app published by Google is available to consumers, via the Play Store: https://play.google.com/store/apps/details?d=com.google.android.projection.gearhead.
This app is necessary for connecting the driver's Android phone (running a Lollipop/5.0 or newer OS) to their *Android Auto* compatible head-unit in their car. As an *Android Auto* developer, in order to connect your Android development phone to your *Android Auto head unit emulator*, you will need to install the *Android Auto* app on your Android development device.

Android Auto App, Installation

You may install the *Android Auto App* via your browser while signed into Google and choose the Android phone or tablet device, that you intend to use for development.

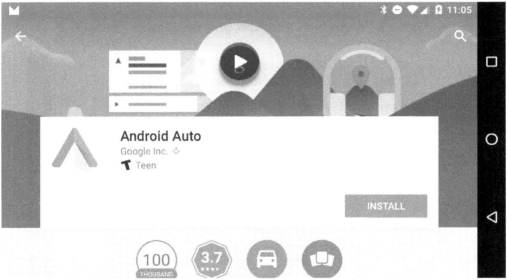

Figure **3-6** Play Store App Listing - *Android Auto App*

Alternately, you may start the *Play Store* App on your Android development phone or tablet device, search for the term "Android Auto", identify the correct app and perform the installation steps. I used the latter approach, as Figure **3-6** indicates.

Figure **3-7A** *Android Auto* app, post installation, first run

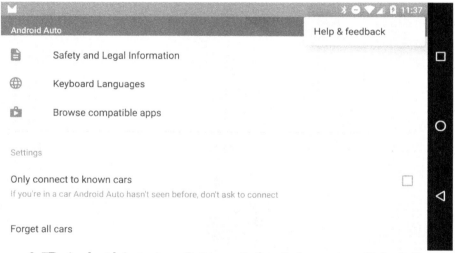
Figure **3-7B** *Android Auto* App, Settings, Safety Information, Help & Feedback

For the purpose of software development, you will need to ensure that the option *Only Connect to known cars* – seen in Figure **3-7B** – is left unchecked (in order to permit your phone to establish the handshake with head-units more readily). It is important to take a moment to get familiar with the various headings of content and options such as *Safety and Legal Information* and *Help and Feedback*.

Android Auto App, Enabling Developer Mode

In order to enable *Developer Mode* for *Android Auto*, you will need to tap 10 times on the words *Android Auto* on the top action bar (Figures 3-7C and 3-7D).

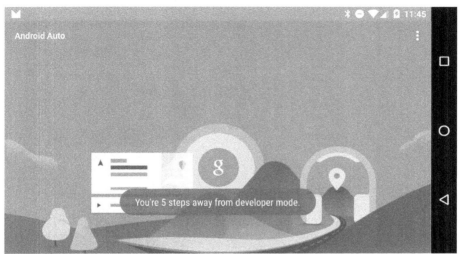

Figure **3-7C** *Android Auto App*, enabling Developer mode, by tapping on the logo

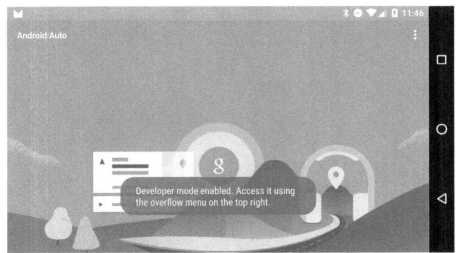

Figure **3-7D** *Android Auto App*, post Developer mode enabled

This tapping routine for enabling *Developer mode* in *Android Auto* is obviously very similar to the process for enabling *Developer mode* for an Android phone device (*Settings*

→ *About phone* → *Build number* <taps....>).

Figure **3-7E** Overflow menu options, post developer mode enablement

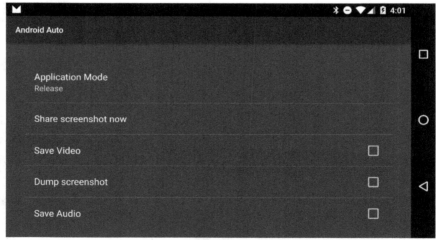
Figure **3-8A** Android Auto app/ Developer Settings

After enabling *Developer mode* in the *Android Auto App*, you will find that several overflow menu items including *Developer settings* and *Start head unit server* become available (Figure 3-7E). You also see the *Quit developer mode* item, which can turn off *Developer mode*. You can re-enable *Developer mode* at any time, by performing the tapping routine all over again.

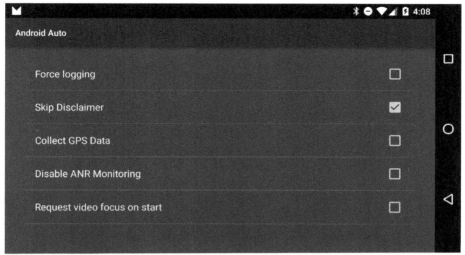

Figure **3-8B** *Android Auto App/* Developer Settings (continued)

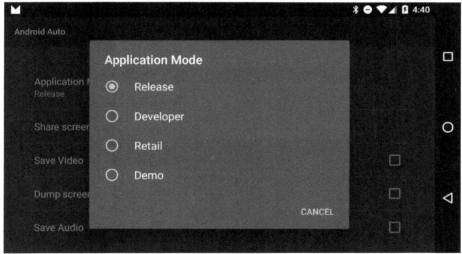

Figure **3-8C** *Android Auto App/* Developer Settings/ Application Mode

Accessing the *Developer settings* item in the over flow menu (Figure 3-7E) will take you to the screens shown in Figures 3-8A and 3-8B. The only top level setting that I found enabled by default – at the time of writing – was the *Skip Disclaimer* item. *Application mode* – the topmost option in *Developer settings* – presents several options such as *Release, Developer, Retail,* and *Demo.* I left the selected default option *Release* untouched for now (Figure 3-8C). At the time of writing, these developer options are still evolving.

Running the *Android Auto Head Unit Emulator*

Firstly, you will need to ensure that your phone is connected via USB to your development computer.

Starting the Head Unit Server *(on your Android phone)*

You will need to start the Head unit server, via the overflow menu item seen in Figure 3-7E. You should see a notification on the top left of your Android phone device, and upon accessing it, you should see the open notification drawer showing *Android Auto Developer/Head unit server running* (Figure 3-9).

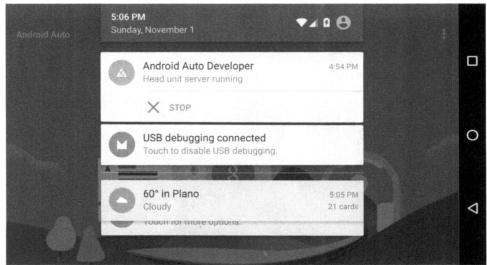

Figure **3-9** *Android Auto App/* Head unit server running

This notification is persistent – as long as the *Head unit server* is running, you should see its notification icon at the top left of your device. You will also notice the "workman with a spade" icon – suggesting road work – which serves to indicate that the *Android Auto App/Head unit server* is currently not connected to the *Android Auto* head-unit emulator.

ADB port forwarding (Development computer)

The *Desktop head unit* (emulator) program will need to connect to the *Head unit server* running on the phone device, via the Android debug bridge (*adb*). When you enable Development mode on your Android phone device – something we did not cover in this chapter – (via *Settings → About Phone → Build number* and tapping on the build number), that causes the **adbd** process to start on the phone and monitor USB connections for *adb* server connection from the other end of USB connection, on your Development computer.

```
- $ adb shell ps | grep adbd
shell     1713    1     5784    268                    00000000 R /sbin/adbd
- $
```

Figure **3-10A** adbd process running on Android phone

```
- $ ps -eaf | grep adb | grep -v grep
sanjay    17304   1561   0 10:21 ?        00:00:41 adb -P 5037 fork-server server
- $
```

Figure **3-10B** adb server process running on my Linux Development host

Adb port forwarding refers to the forwarding of socket connections from a local port to a remote port. The syntax is *forward <local> <remote>*. Because the two ADB processes are bridged across the Development computer and the phone device, the forward command is easily coordinated between them. The following command typed into the terminal of my development computer setup adb port forwarding:

```
$ adb forward tcp:5277 tcp:5277
```

Starting the Android Auto Desktop Head unit emulator (DHU)

If you have completed the steps so far, including the adb forward step shown above, you are ready to start the head-unit emulator. The Desktop Head Unit (head-unit emulator) runs on your development computer and emulates a in-vehicle *Android Auto* head-unit, thereby making it possible to develop Android apps without needing a real in-vehicle head unit. As the *Android Auto* head-unit is a projection standard, rather than a full fledged Android OS flavor for the in-vehicle infotainment system, the term AVD does not apply – at the time of writing – to the *Android Auto* emulator.

Starting the DHU can be accomplished simply by running the *desktop-head-unit* program located in the directory *<ANDROID_SDK_LOCATION>/extras/google/auto/*. The DHU cannot and will not start unless *adb port forwarding* has been setup and the *Head Unit Server* is running on your Android phone.

```
— $ desktop-head-unit
ALSA lib pcm c:2239:(snd_pcm_open_noupdate) Unknown PCM cards.pcm rear
ALSA lib pcm c:2239:(snd_pcm_open_noupdate) Unknown PCM cards.pcm center_lfe
ALSA lib pcm c:2239:(snd_pcm_open_noupdate) Unknown PCM cards.pcm side
ALSA lib pcm_route.c:947:(find_matching_chmap) Found no matching channel map
bt_audio_service_open: connect() failed: Connection refused (111)
bt_audio_service_open: connect() failed: Connection refused (111)
bt_audio_service_open: connect() failed: Connection refused (111)
bt_audio_service_open: connect() failed: Connection refused (111)
Cannot connect to server socket err = No such file or directory
Cannot connect to server request channel
jack server is not running or cannot be started
Connecting over ADB to localhost:5277...connected.
>
```

Figure **3-11** Starting the *Android Auto Desktop Head unit emulator (DHU)*

Figure **3-12** DHU, waiting for phone

Figure 3-11 shows the output of running the *desktop-head-unit* program on my Linux development computer. (Although the output of the *desktop-head-unit* program on my system shows errors and warnings, they were evidently of no consequence, as I soon found out.) Figure 3-12 shows the DHU screen that may be briefly seen while the DHU is waiting to establish the connection with the Head-unit server running on the phone. Once the head-unit and the phone establish their connection, the head-unit displays the *Android Auto* head unit user interface (Figure 3-13).

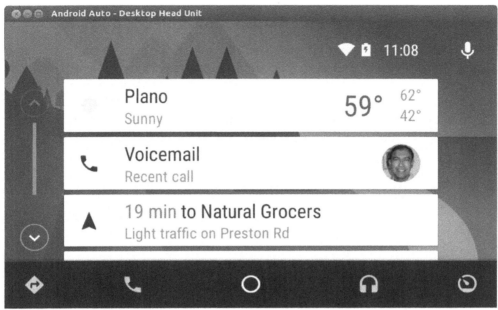
Figure **3-13** Desktop Head Unit (emulator) started !

Figure **3-14** Phone in *Android Auto* mode/ screen lock

Once the head-unit connects to the phone successfully, the phone in turn loses its touch screen responsiveness and displays the black and white *Android Auto* screen lock (Figure 3-14). Simultaneously, the head-unit commences to serve as the primary means of driver interaction. The user's current location, recent places visited, and recent communications, that are generally available via the phone become available via the head unit's screen. This type of interaction represents a user centric and device independent model of interaction.

Desktop Head Unit, Head-unit Server, and Projection System

Under the covers, the DHU program connects via the *adb* port forwarding mechanism to the *Head-unit server* that is (needs to be) running on the Android phone. The *Head-unit server* in turn, upon receiving the connection from the DHU, triggers the start of the *projection_system* service. The *projection_system* which is a service that runs as a separate process in turn drives the visual user experience and interaction onto the DHU running on the development computer, via the Head-unit server and the *adb* connection (Figure 3-15).

```
~ $ adb shell ps | grep gearhead
u0_a88    13815 3255   967012 79900 SyS_epoll_ 0000000000 S com.google.android.
projection.gearhead
u0_a88    14056 3255   916460 35836 SyS_epoll_ 0000000000 S com.google.android.
projection.gearhead:projection_system
~ $
```

Figure **3-15** *Android Auto App* processes running on Android phone

The *adb server* which runs in the background, on the development computer, serves adb clients. With adb port forwarding in place, the adb server is also able to serve the DHU over the adb port forwarding mechanism via a two way connectivity established between the DHU and the *Head-unit server* and the Projection System.

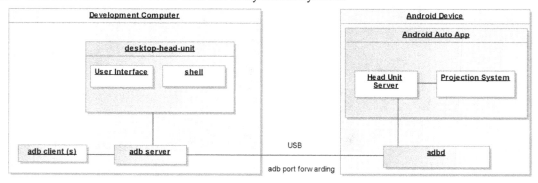

Figure 3-16 DHU, Head-unit Server, and Projection System

Figure 3-16 shows a representative diagram of the connectivity between the desktop-head-unit (DHU) and *adb* server running on the development computer, with the adbd process and the *Head-unit server* and the Projection system that are running on the Android device via the adb port forwarding mechanism.

Desktop Head Unit : User Interface

The most common form of *Android Auto*-compatible head-units – in the real world – are touch screen based. The DHU (emulator) mimics a touch screen based *Android Auto* head-unit.

Most desktops and many laptop development computers today lack touch screen support. In case you happen to use a touch screen based laptop or desktop as your development computer, you can interact with the DHU via touch. In case you use a non-touch screen based development computer, you can simulate touches by using mouse clicks.

Android Auto head-unit's user interface includes an action bar at the bottom, with the five icons representing – from left to right -- driving directions, telephony, Home, Music, and the access to the native head-unit interface. The status bar on the top shows the battery status and signal strength indicators of your connected Android phone – not the head unit which serves merely as a projection medium for the connected Android phone. The DHU provides a realistic emulation of the in-vehicle *Android Auto* user experience which makes it possible to more easily understand the basics of the platform.

Driving Directions/Maps

Directions and maps are central to driving and driving directions. Voice based, hands-free input is central to minimization of distraction and driver safety. Once the voice interface is active, you may speak out your destination, in order to get access to driving directions (Figures 3-17A, 3-17B, and 3-17C).

The voice based interface can be triggered via clicking the microphone icon – or touching your development computer's touch screen, if available – seen on the top right of the above screen. (Figure 3-17B).

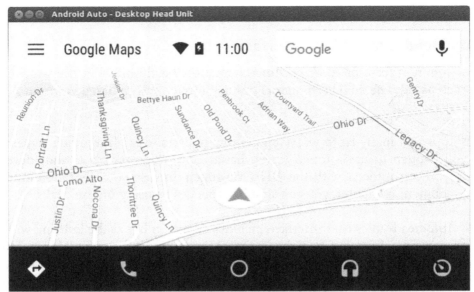

Figure **3-17A** DHU Maps

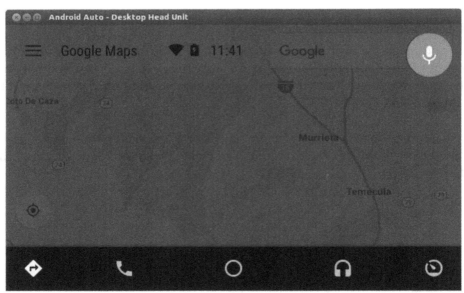

Figure **3-17B** DHU Maps, microphone active

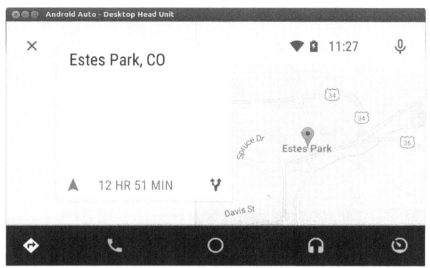

Figure **3-17C** DHU Maps, destination input via voice

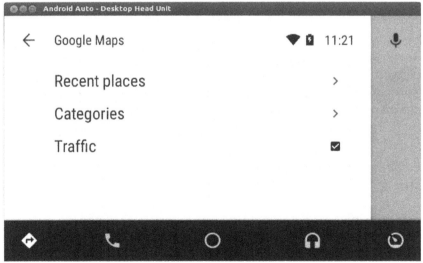

Figure **3-18A** DHU Maps, Navigation Drawer

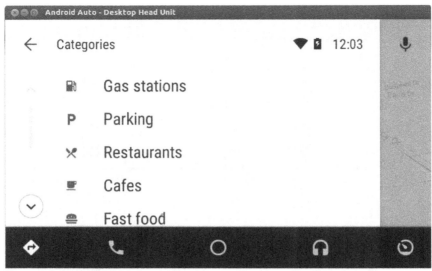

Figure **3-18B** DHU Maps, Navigation Drawer, Destination Categories

The navigation drawer on the top left of the main Google Maps screen shown in Figure 3-17A provides access to items such as recent places and categories of business or service locations such as gas stations, ATM locations, restaurants, parking, and hospitals (Figures 3-18A and 3-18B).

A setting such as *Traffic* – when enabled – will result in the navigation to factor in the live traffic conditions when computing the driving duration and estimating destination arrival time. It happens to be enabled by default, but the user has the ability to toggle the setting. The ability to easily choose parking, gas stations, restaurants, and fast food locations is integrated into maps and driving directions.

Telephony

Accessing Telephony via the phone icon on the bottom action bar displays a few recent or much contacted contacts (Figure 3-19A).

This makes it possible to conveniently and safely make phone calls with minimal distraction from the activity of driving. The left navigation drawer on the top left provides access to voice mail, the dialer, call history and missed calls (Figure 3-19B).

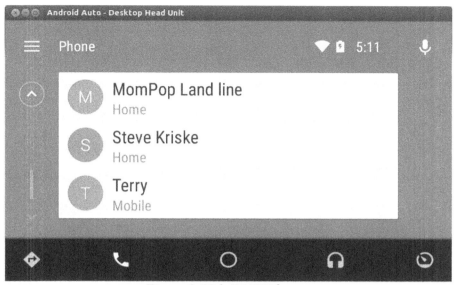
Figure **3-19A** DHU Phone

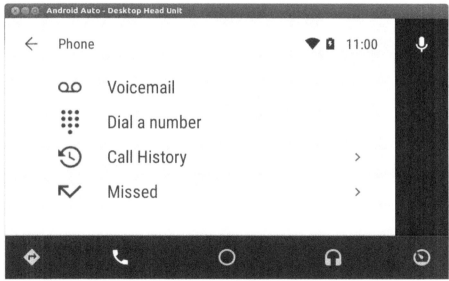
Figure **3-19B** DHU Phone, top left navigation drawer items

You will notice from comparing the map and phone functions, that the user interfaces are consistent so as to be predictable with respect to look and feel and behavior – so as to be minimally distracting.

Although mobile apps in general benefit from the principles of simplicity, consistency, and ease of use, there is also an element of surprise that hand-held apps might introduce in order to impress the users and engage their attention. However, in case of the automobile, the nature of the automobile experience and the seriousness of driving necessitate that particular design and interaction principles be followed. The *Android Auto* platform enforces such restrictions, at many levels in various ways – as covered in subsequent chapters.

Home

The home screen with very limited content gets displayed when the user/driver connects the Android phone to the car's head-unit.

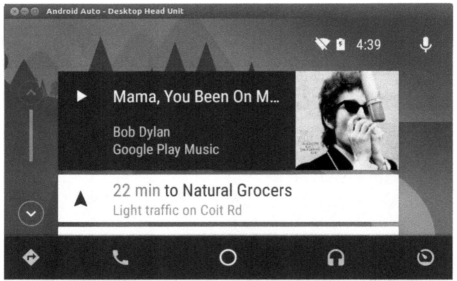

Figure **3-20** *Android Auto* Head-unit Home screen

The circle icon provides access to the Auto home screen (Figure 3-20), which presents various suggestion cards. Figure 3-20 for example, shows two suggestion cards – a song the user might care to play, and a driving destination that the user is likely to need to drive to. You will notice that – unlike an Android phone's Home screen – the *Android Auto* head-unit Home screen has very few actions and choices.

Music

You will need at least one audio/music app that has been extended to *Android Auto* installed on your phone. Google Play Music is one such app and the best choice for getting started with *Android Auto*. For me, accessing the Music/ headphone icon engaged *Google Play Music* on the head-unit screen.

Google Play Music

Google Play Music is Google's online music vault and streaming service, which allows users to upload their music collection. Google Play Music users have access to their music collection via their *Android Auto* head-unit.

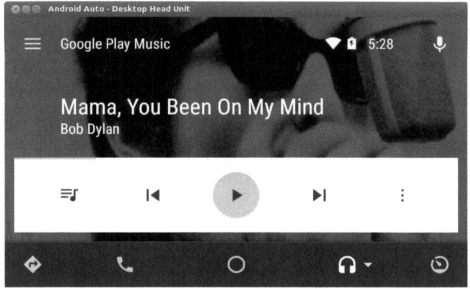

Figure **3-21A** Music/ Google Play Music

Also, the user's context and most recently played song – even if played via some other device than the head-unit – gets displayed so users can pick up from where they had left off.

In my case, accessing Google Play Music via the head-unit displayed the song I had recently played via the desktop.

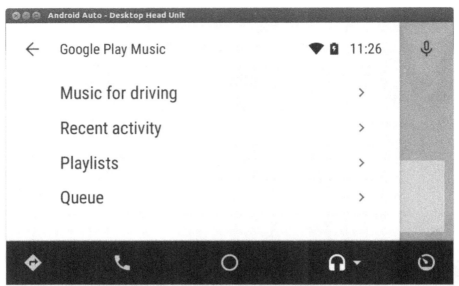

Figure **3-21B** Google Play Music, left navigation drawer items

The left navigation drawer on the top left provides access to the user's own play lists, queues, recent activity, and music for driving (Figure 3-21B).

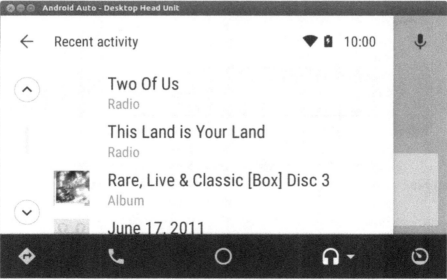

Figure **3-21C** Google Play Music, recent activity

Figure 3-21C shows the recent activity information. Other drawer items such as play lists and queues are left for you to explore. They are fairly obvious, simple, and predictable.

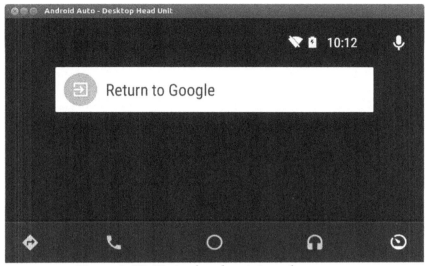

Figure **3-22** Native head-unit interface access

Head-unit Native Interface

The icon at the extreme right of the bottom bar is suggestive of an odometer or fuel gauge and provides access to the head-unit's native interface. Touching this icon displays a screen (Figure 3-22) that displays an icon and the text "Return to Google". Attempting to access "Return to Google" has no effect in the DHU.

On the real head-unit that supports *Android Auto*, the equivalent item will take you to the native infotainment system. As *Android Auto* is merely a projection standard, there is typically a two way access from *Android Auto* → native and from native → *Android Auto*. There are functions that may exist in the "native" system that are not available in *Android Auto*. We will be covering more specifics in this arena, in Chapter 5 - On the Road which is dedicated to the in-vehicle *Android Auto* experience including the native head-unit user experience.

Desktop Head Unit (DHU) Command Shell

The *desktop-head-unit* tool besides starting the user interface which we covered in the preceding section, also provides a command shell. DHU commands support application validation and testing via controlling the emulator's behavior to mimic real world scenarios such as day and night display modes and playing voice commands. Figure 3-23 shows the output of the *help* command which lists all the available DHU shell commands.

```
Connecting over ADB to localhost:5277...connected.
> help
Android Auto - Desktop Head Unit
  Build: 2015-09-16-2258745
  Version: 1.0-linux

The available commands are:
        Controller:
                "dpad up" "dpad down" "dpad left" "dpad right" "dpad click" "dpad b
ack" "dpad soft left" "dpad soft right" "dpad rotate left" "dpad flick left" "dpad
rotate right" "dpad flick right"
        Day/Night Sensor:
                "night" "day" "daynight" "nightday"
        Microphone:
                "mic begin" "mic play" "mic repeat"
        System:
                "help" "quit" "exit" "licenses" "sleep" "screenshot"
        Touch:
                "tap"
>
```

Figure **3-23** desktop-head-unit command line shell, *help* output

For instance, issuing the *night* command by typing into the DHU prompt, will cause the display to switch to night mode – with a dark background (Figure 3-24). In day mode, the display uses high brightness and full color. In night mode, the display uses high contrast and low brightness. The *night* command can be really useful for getting a sense of how your application's user interface might look like in night mode.

In a real vehicle, the ambient light as detected by the vehicle's light sensor is used to determine the display mode. Low light conditions typically trigger the turning on of the headlights (headlight auto mode) and simultaneously, the head-unit display's switching into night mode. In many vehicles, turning on the head lights manually will also result in the head-unit's display to acquire the night mode.

Figure **3-24** *Android Auto* Head-unit in night mode

The high level DHU command categories and commands are listed below:

Category	Description	Commands
Controller	Some head-units models use a rotary control for input. The Controller category of commands simulates user input actions such as pressing and rotating the rotary controller. In order to mimic head-units that use a controller, you will need to start the head-unit emulator using the command : *desktop-head-unit -i controller* The emulator started with the option will fail to respond to touch events or mouse clicks. But it will respond to the dpad commands such as *dpad click*	*dpad* (with subcommands such as *click*, *left*, *right*, *up*, *down,...*) (no arguments)
Day Night Sensor	In a real vehicle, the ambient light as detected by the light sensor determines the head-unit's day or night display mode. The Day Night Sensor category of commands allow you to toggle the day / night mode, or set it to a particular mode.	night, *day*, *daynight*, *nightday* (no arguments)

Microphone	Many vehicle models have steering wheel buttons to trigger microphone input. Some drivers find this mechanism more convenient than tapping on the head-unit microphone. The Microphone family of commands provides microphone control.	*mic* (with subcommands such as *begin*, *play*, and *repeat* plus arguments as applicable)
Touch	The Touch family of commands simulates touch.	*tap* (with arguments for co-ordinates in the X and Y axis)
System	The System category of command include trivial commands, including help and exit	*help*, *quit*, *exit*, *licenses*, *sleep* and *screenshot*.

You might notice that there are no commands to simulate your current location, for instance. The Android AVD emulator (not the DHU emulator) currently – at the time of writing – does not include the *Android Auto App* nor the *Play Store app--* using which other apps available on the *Play Store* can be installed. This limitation necessitates the use of a real Android Phone device with the *Android Auto App* installed in order to connect to the DHU.

Google is expected to develop more sophisticated Android AVD emulators that will include the Play Store App and therefore have the ability to install – at least some, if not all/any – Play Store published Apps on to the AVD emulator.

The Android AVD emulator is a powerful tool that has advantages over a physical/hardware Android phone device, for instance the AVD emulator can simulate the current location (by means external to the app) and also set attributes such as the battery level.

Somewhat incidentally, the steps for setting the current location for testing purposes, on an Android AVD emulator – by connecting to the emulator via *telnet* and issuing the *geo* command – are shown in Figure 3-25.

While on the subject of simulating the current location – something of interest for *Android Auto* development – the Android SDK informally provides a permission *android.permission. ACCESS_MOCK_LOCATION* which can be useful for testing location based Apps in conjunction with the LocationManager's setTestProviderLocation method. The LocationManager's setTestLocationProvider allows you to programatically set the location in debug mode for purposes of testing. More details can be found at: http://developer.android.com/reference/android/location/LocationManager.html#setTestProviderLocation

```
~ $ adb devices
List of devices attached
emulator-5554   device

~ $ telnet localhost 5554
Trying 127.0.0.1...
Connected to localhost.
Escape character is '^]'.
Android Console: type 'help' for a list of commands
OK
geo fix 37.19 -122.16
OK
```

Figure **3-25** Simulating current location using geo fix command (Android AVD emulator)

Desktop Head Unit (DHU) Scripting

The Desktop Head Unit supports running a sequence of commands as a script. The *desktop-head-unit* command can be fed the DHU command sequence, using I/O redirection. DHU scripts can be useful for testing, automation and demos.

The script *overview/browseBottomBar.dhu* which is available as part of this book's sample code uses the *tap*, sleep and *screenshot* commands to simulate taps to browse/access the various DHU features at a high level, namely - maps, phone, home, music and native head-unit, and output the various corresponding screen shots as *png* files.

The *tap* command used in this script, requires the x and y offsets (with respect to the top left corner of the DHU screen) as arguments. It was fairly easy to determine the x and y offsets for the various icons and regions of interest on the screen, with a little trial and error, in the absence of any formal documentation that I could find at the time of writing. I determined that the DHU screen measures about 500 x 800, on my development computer running the Linux version of the desktop-head-unit.

The *screenshot* command can be used for capturing the progress of the application and user interfaces, during the progression of automated scripts and user interfaces. The command requires the output file name as the argument. The content of this script is shown below in it's entirety:

```
 sleep 5
tap 45 460
 sleep 1
 screenshot maps.png
 sleep 5
tap 180 460
 sleep 1
 screenshot phone.png
 sleep 5
tap 400 460
 sleep 1
 screenshot home.png
 sleep 5
tap 580 460
 sleep 1
 screenshot music.png
 sleep 5
tap 750 460
 sleep 1
 screenshot native.png
 sleep 5
exit
```

The above script can be executed via the command line of your development computer, as shown below:

```
$ desktop-head-unit < browseBottomBar.dhu
```

The effect of running this script is the DHU interface undergoes changes due to the screen taps that the script initiates and the output of the corresponding screen shots:

```
~/github/autosource/scripts/overview $ ls *png
home.png maps.png music.png native.png phone.png
```

The *mic* command makes it possible to activate the microphone and provide voice based input from a audio file that you have pre-recorded for testing. Also, there are several off-the-shelf audio sample files that are part of the Android SDK DHU extras, and these are located under: <ANDROID_SDK_HOME>/extras/google/auto/voice/ :

```
exitnav.wav
navgoogle.wav
navsoh.wav
nextturn.wav
showalternateroute.wav
howlong.wav
navhome.wav
navwork.wav
pause.wav
showtraffic.wav
```

There are several more scripts that pertain to phone calls, music playback, and navigation, that are included in the source code for this book.

We covered in this chapter, the steps of getting setup and familiarized with the Android Auto head-unit emulator(DHU), Android SDK stand-alone tools and Android Studio 2.0/Preview IDE. We also covered the DHU's maps, phone, and music functions as well as the DHU commands.

References and further reading

https://en.wikipedia.org/wiki/Apache_Harmony
http://www.oracle.com/technetwork/java/javase/overview/index.html
http://www.oracle.com/technetwork/java/javase/downloads/jdk8-downloads-2133151.html
http://gradle.org
http://developer.android.com/sdk/installing/index.html.
https://en.wikipedia.org/wiki/Telnet
http://tools.android.com/tech-docs/instant-run
http://developer.android.com/training/auto/start/index.html
https://developer.android.com/tools/help/desktop-head-unit.html
https://developer.android.com/tools/help/desktop-head-unit.html#cmd-bindings
http://developer.android.com/tools/help/avd-manager.html
http://developer.android.com/reference/android/location/LocationManager.html#setTestProvider
Location
http://tools.android.com/tech-docs/instant-run
http://openjdk.java.net/projects/mobile/android.html
http://venturebeat.com/2015/12/29/google-confirms-next-android-version-wont-use-oracles-proprietary-java-apis
https://en.wikipedia.org/wiki/GNU_General_Public_License
http://tools.android.com/download/studio/builds/2-0-preview

CHAPTER 4   Hello Auto

Finally, all is set for us to commence writing our first *Android Auto* application. This chapter covers the hands-on steps for doing so, without getting deep into the underlying APIs and theory aspects, which are covered in subsequent chapters. The associated source code is available in it's entirety as part of the source code for this book.

Hello Auto(Base)

We will first cover a simple "base" application(*HelloAutoB*), that is not enabled for *Android Auto*. The application allows the user to set an alarm for a future time. When the alarm triggers, an application component originates a simple notification. Once we have verified that this base application is working as intended, we will subsequently extend it to the *Android Auto* platform. This approach mirrors the typical real world scenario, wherein an existing Android application's particular features are identified as being relevant for extension into *Android Auto*. In the real world, few apps will be suitable for extension into the *Android Auto* platform (due to factors such as relevance to driving and safety).

Hello Auto(B) - software components and artifacts

This application is targeted for API level 23 (Android 6/Marshmallow). It has two Android components, namely the *AlarmSetterActivity* and *MyAlarmBroadcastReceiver* classes which have entries in the *AndroidManifest.xml* as indicated in the snippet below:

```
<activity
 android:name=".AlarmSetterActivity"
 android:label="@string/app_name"
 android:theme="@style/AppTheme.NoActionBar">
 <intent-filter>
 <action android:name="android.intent.action.MAIN" />
 <category android:name="android.intent.category.LAUNCHER" />
 </intent-filter>
</activity>

<receiver android:name=".MyAlarmBroadcastReceiver" >
</receiver>
```

AlarmSetterActivity provides the user with a button (layout xml not included among the snippets) that sets the alarm which fires after exactly 3 minutes. The alarm in turn uses a *PendingIntent* to engage the *MyAlarmBroadcastReceiver*. The *setAlarm* method invokes the Android framework's *AlarmManager*'s *setExact* method to set the alarm and engage the *MyAlarmBroadcastReceiver* via a *PendingIntent*. (In real world applications, exact alarms should be avoided for efficiency reasons. Inexact alarms are preferable as they incur less resource overhead.) The implementation of the *setAlarm* method which gets called when the alarm button is touched, is shown in the snippet below:

```
private void setAlarm () {
 Log.d (TAG, "setAlarm()...") ;
 operationPendingIntent =
PendingIntent.getBroadcast(getApplicationContext(),0, new
Intent(getApplicationContext(),MyAlarmBroadcastReceiver.class),0);
 alarmManager= (AlarmManager) getSystemService(Context.ALARM_SERVICE);
 alarmManager.setExact(AlarmManager.ELAPSED_REALTIME_WAKEUP,
 SystemClock.elapsedRealtime()+3*SECONDS_IN_MINUTE*MILLIS_IN_A_SECOND,
 operationPendingIntent);
 Log.d (TAG, "setAlarm() setExact alarm for 3 minutes later...") ;
}
```

MyAlarmBroadcastReceiver's *onReceive* method invokes the *originateSimpleNotification* method which encapsulates the operations for originating a notification and entails using the Android system's *NotificationManager,* as shown in the snippet below:

```
@Override
 public void onReceive(Context context, Intent intent) {
  int referenceId = (int) SystemClock.elapsedRealtime() ;
   String messageTitle = "HelloAuto" ;
   String messageContent = "HelloAuto Alarm was Triggered at " + new Date();
   Log.d (TAG, "onReceive()... " + referenceId) ;
   originateSimpleNotification(context, referenceId, messageTitle,
                                          messageContent);
 }
private void originateSimpleNotification (Context context, int referenceId,
   String messageTitle, String messageContent) {
   Notification notification = new Notification.Builder(context)
       .setSmallIcon(R.drawable.alarm36)
       .setContentTitle(messageTitle)
       .setContentText(messageContent)
       .setColor(context.getResources().getColor(R.color.colorPrimary))
       .build();
 NotificationManager notificationManager = (NotificationManager)
              context.getSystemService(Context.NOTIFICATION_SERVICE);
 notificationManager.notify(referenceId, notification);
}
```

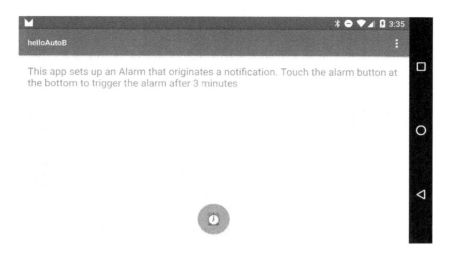

Figure **4-1A** HelloAutoB application main screen

Hello Auto(B), running

Figure 4-1A shows the app's main screen that includes the button that sets the alarm for 3 minutes. Upon touching the alarm button, you will see a small message at the bottom of the screen indicating that the alarm has been set for 3 minutes hence. (Figure 4-1B).

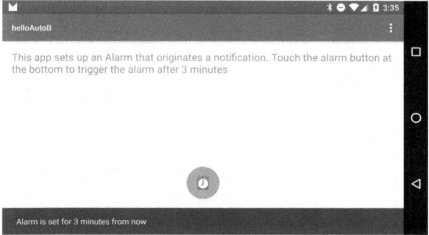

Figure **4-1B** HelloAutoB application, alarm set

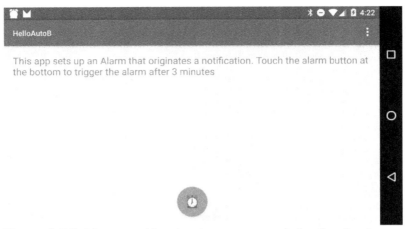

Figure **4-1C** Alarm notification icon seen top left, after 3 minutes

After exactly 3 minutes have elapsed, you should see a notification with an alarm icon on the device's status bar on the top left. Figure 4-1C shows such a notification on the extreme left of the notification bar on my device. Upon expanding the notification drawer by touching the notification, the content of the notification, ie. "*Hello Auto/ HelloAuto Alarm was triggered at ...*" are displayed as shown in Figure 4-1D. The app does not need to be running after setting the alarm, in order for the alarm to trigger and the notification to fire (as we have engaged the Android system's *AlarmManager* service).

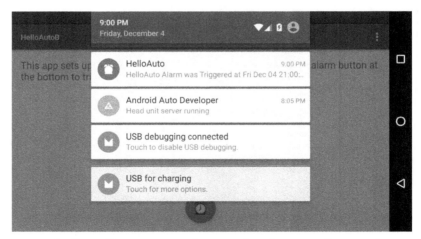

Figure **4-1D** HelloAutoB notification detail, in notification drawer

Before we work on extending this app to engage with the *Android Auto* platform, let us see for ourselves experimentally, whether this notification currently propagates to the head-unit emulator(DHU). First, I ran the *Android Auto App* and started the *Head unit server* via the overflow menu action. The corresponding figure has not been shown here, as we have covered this step in Chapter 3 (Figure 3-7E and Figure 3-9).

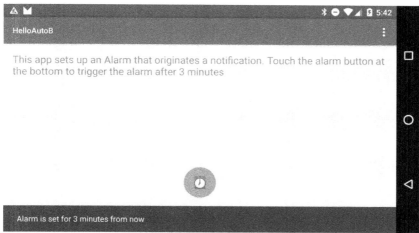

Figure **4-2A** *HelloAutoB* app, after Android Auto App's Head-unit server was started

Next, I started the *HelloAutoB* app again and set the 3 minute alarm. You will notice the notification at the top left (workman with a spade icon) which indicates that the *Head unit server* is running, but not connected to a DHU (Figure 4-2A).

After that, I started the DHU on my development computer by executing the following commands :

```
$ adb forward tcp:5277 tcp:5277
$ desktop-head-unit
```

Figure 4-2B shows the home screen of the DHU, upon starting it. (The effects of the *adb forward* command are transient and the command will need to be executed every time you engage in an *Android Auto* development session, and/or disconnect or re-connect the USB cable between your Android phone and development computer.) I waited for over 3 minutes and did not see any notification in the DHU. This is to be expected, as our app is not enabled for *Android Auto,* as yet.

Upon exiting the DHU, my Android phone device displayed the *HelloAuto* notification that happened to be triggered while the phone was in Auto mode, but displayed only after exiting Auto mode(Figure 4-2C). This confirms that the app's alarm and notification functioned, although the app was not running. Conducting this experiment is quite relevant, as we will be repeating these very steps after enhancing this application to extend it to *Android Auto*.

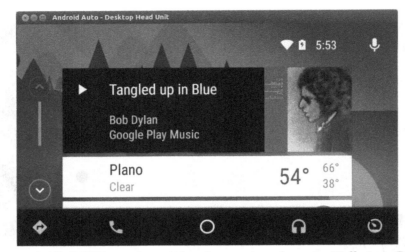

Figure **4-2B** DHU running, right after setting alarm in *HelloAutoB* app

Hello Auto(Auto), enabling *Android Auto*

The key class that supports extending notifications into the *Android Auto* platform is the *CarExtender* which is a static inner class that was added to *android.app.Notification* in API level 23. The *Notification.CarExtender.UnreadConversation* class is in turn is a static inner class that encapsulates the messages/ conversations. Details of *CarExtender* can be found at the following API references:

https://developer.android.com/reference/android/app/Notification.CarExtender.html
http://developer.android.com/reference/android/app/PendingIntent.html
http://developer.android.com/reference/android/app/RemoteInput.html

When using *CarExtender*, the display characteristics of the notification ie. the attributes of the notification such as content, text size, colors and associated icons, will need to be set specifically for *Android Auto*. The generic notification attributes that apply to hand-held devices are not used for the notification that is extended to *Android Auto* — as the user interfaces displayed via *Android Auto* have unique and very specific design requirements, display criteria, and constraints. We will be covering more details on this in subsequent chapters.

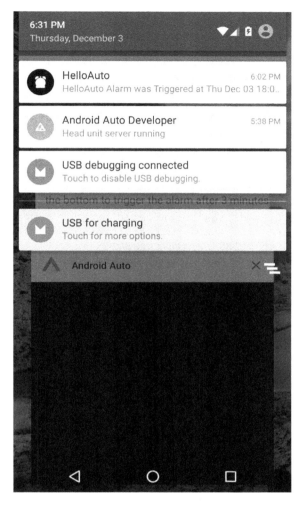

Figure **4-2C** *HelloAuto* notification on phone after exiting the DHU

Hello Auto(A), engaging the CarExtender

In order to extend the application to *Android Auto*, I first copied over the *HelloAutoB* (base) app as the starting point for the *HelloAutoA* (Auto) app which we will shortly go about modifying. The "A" app has the same package name and application id (*applicationId "info.androidautobook.helloauto"*) as the earlier "B" app; therefore the "A" app when installed on the same device can end up replacing/clobbering the "B" app. I added a method *originateCarExtendedNotification* to the *MyAlarmBroadcastReceiver* class and called it from the *onMessage* implementation, as shown in the snippet below:

```java
@Override
public void onReceive(Context context, Intent intent) {
 int referenceId = (int) SystemClock.elapsedRealtime() ;
 String messageTitle = "HelloAuto" ;
 String messageContent = "HelloAuto Alarm was Triggered at "
                                            + new Date() ;
 Log.d (TAG, "onReceive() NCT... " + referenceId) ;
 originateCarExtendedNotification(context, referenceId, messageTitle,
            messageContent);}

private void originateCarExtendedNotification (Context context,
        int referenceId, String messageTitle, String messageContent) {
 PendingIntent readPendingIntent = PendingIntent.getBroadcast(context,
        referenceId,
        new Intent().addFlags(Intent.FLAG_INCLUDE_STOPPED_PACKAGES)
        .setAction(ACTION_READ).putExtra("reference_id", referenceId),
         PendingIntent.FLAG_UPDATE_CURRENT);
 RemoteInput remoteInput = new RemoteInput.Builder(EXTRA_VOICE_REPLY)
        .setLabel(messageTitle)
        .build();
 PendingIntent replyIntent = PendingIntent.getBroadcast(context,
      referenceId,
      new Intent().addFlags(Intent.FLAG_INCLUDE_STOPPED_PACKAGES)
      .setAction(REPLY_ACTION).putExtra("conversation_id", referenceId),
      PendingIntent.FLAG_UPDATE_CURRENT);
 Notification.CarExtender.Builder unReadConversationsBuilder =
            new Notification.CarExtender.Builder(messageTitle) ;
 unReadConversationsBuilder.addMessage(messageContent);

unReadConversationsBuilder.setLatestTimestamp(System.currentTimeMillis()
                                                      ) ;
 unReadConversationsBuilder.setReadPendingIntent(readPendingIntent) ;
 unReadConversationsBuilder.setReplyAction(replyIntent, remoteInput);
 Log.d (TAG, "originateCarExtendedNotification() carExtender") ;
 Notification.CarExtender carExtender = new Notification.CarExtender() ;
 carExtender.setColor(context.getResources().getColor(
                                        R.color.colorPrimary));
 carExtender.setLargeIcon(BitmapFactory.decodeResource(
                     context.getResources(), R.drawable.alarm36)) ;
 carExtender.setUnreadConversation(unReadConversationsBuilder.build()) ;
 Log.d (TAG, "originateCarExtendedNotification() carExtender="+
        carExtender) ;
 Notification notification = new Notification.Builder(context)
        .setSmallIcon(R.drawable.alarm36)
        .setContentTitle (messageTitle)
        .setContentText(messageContent)
        .setContentIntent(readPendingIntent)
        .setColor(context.getResources().getColor(R.color.colorPrimary))
```

```
        .extend(carExtender)
        .build() ;
Log.d (TAG,"originateCarExtendedNotification()
                              notification="+notification);
NotificationManager notificationManager = (NotificationManager)
              context.getSystemService(Context.NOTIFICATION_SERVICE);
notificationManager.notify(referenceId, notification);
}
```

CarExtender, UnreadConversation, explanation

This set of code additions entail the instantiation of *CarExtender.UnreadConversation* and *CarExtender,* which encapsulate the message content and display characteristics. The *extend()* method available in the *NotificationBuilder,* enables the association of the *CarExtender* with the notification. The *RemoteInput* class facilitates input without a keyboard, typically via voice. The *PendingIntent* is an action that can be passed to another application which will execute that action at some future time, on behalf of the originating application. The *CarExtender* becomes operational, with assistance from the *RemoteInput* and *PendingIntent* classes. It is important to associate (non-null) remote input, read pending intent and the reply action with the unread conversation, via method calls *setReadPendingIntent()* and *setReplyAction().*

Another change that needs to be made resides in the *AndroidManifest.xml.* The snippet below shows the addition of the meta-data element to the end of the *AndroidManifest.xml* file :

```
…
 <meta-data android:name="com.google.android.gms.car.application"
       android:resource="@xml/automotive_app_desc"/>
  </application>
</manifest>
```

The content of the *res/xml/automotive_app_desc.xml* file referenced in *AndroidManifest.xml* is shown in the snippet below:

```
<automotiveApp>
   <uses name="notification"/>
</automotiveApp>
```

These changes help declare the current app as an automotive app that is enabled for

Android Auto and engages with Android notifications.

Additionally, I added a broadcast receiver to the code base, the *AndroidManifest.xml* entry for which is shown in the snippet below:

```
<receiver
  android:name=".MessageReadBroadcastReceiver">
  <intent-filter>
  <action
        android:name="info.androidautobook.helloauto.ACTION_READ" />
  </intent-filter>
</receiver>
```

The implementation of the *onMessage()* method for the *MessageReadBroadcastReceiver* clears the notification that was consumed via the head-unit, as is shown in the snippet below:

```
@Override
public void onReceive(Context context, Intent intent) {
  Log.d (TAG, "onReceive()..." + new Date()) ;
  int referenceId = intent.getIntExtra("reference_id", -1);
  if (referenceId > 0) {
  ((NotificationManager)context.getSystemService(
        Context.NOTIFICATION_SERVICE))
      .cancel(referenceId);
  } else {
  Log.w (TAG, "onReceive() could not find notification to cancel") ;
  }
}
```

Hello Auto(A), running

I built this modified (HelloAuto*A*) app and installed it to my Android phone. I verified that the app continued to display the notification on the phone as before without starting the DHU, after 3 minutes of setting the alarm. I then proceeded to repeat the same steps as described earlier in this chapter, of starting the *Android Auto App*, starting the *Head-unit server*, starting the HelloAutoA app, setting the 3 minute alarm and then starting the DHU. Figure 4-3A shows the setting of the 3 minute alarm.

Figure **4-3A** HelloAuto, alarm set

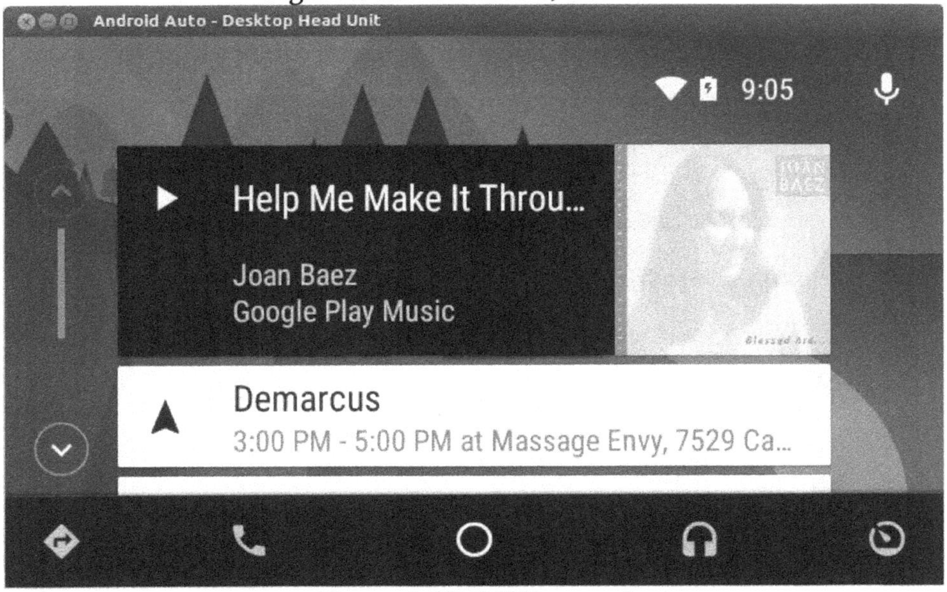

Figure **4-3B** DHU started

Next, I started the DHU immediately (Figure 4-3B) and waited to see if the notification would show up in 3 minutes.

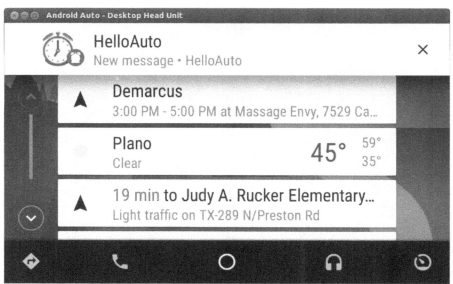
Figure **4-3C** DHU displays notification, 3 minutes after setting the alarm

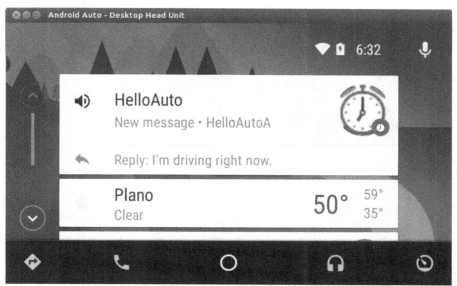
Figure **4-3D** DHU plays the content of the notification, Text To Speech

Figure 4-3C shows the *Hello Auto* notification message as it appeared upon initial delivery in 3 minutes. Figure 4-3D shows the screen transition a few moments later. Tapping on the speaker icon, played the content of the message "Hello Auto Alarm was triggered at ..." as Text-to-Speech (TTS).

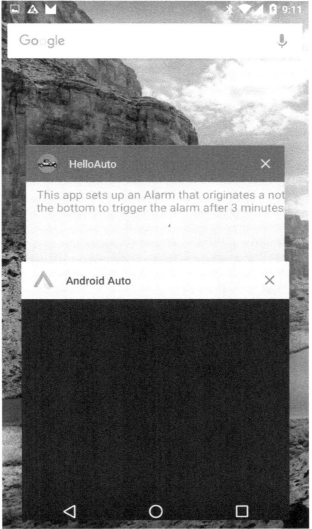

Figure **4-3E** After exiting DHU, notification consumed in DHU, not seen in phone

After exiting the DHU, my phone (Figure 4-3E) did not show any notification --as was to be expected – because the notification had already been consumed via the head-unit based interaction and particularly the application's *MessageReadBroadcastReceiver*'s *onMessage()*

implementation clears the notification. This pattern of application behavior emphasizes the desired user-centric and device-independent approach which has much relevance in a world with a multitude of consumer devices that a given user possesses and interacts with.

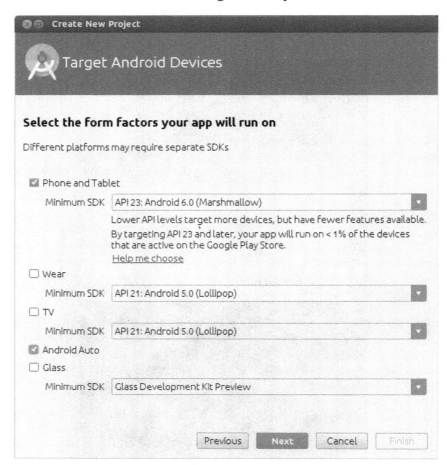

Figure **4-4A** Targeting (extending) an app to *Android Auto*

Android Studio takes care of the snippets needed in the Android manifest file – such as the the <**meta-data**> element – when creating an app and enabling it for the *Android Auto* form factor. Figures 4-4A and 4-4B show the step and effect of targeting an app to the Auto form factor. Figure 4-4A shows the various form factors that an app can be run on (or **extended to,** as is the case for Auto**).** Upon selecting *Android Auto* as a target platform, the subsequent steps of project creation include the selection of either Auto "media" or "messaging", as shown in Figure 4-4B.

Figure **4-4B** An Android Auto app – Media Service, or Messaging Service

In case of a messaging app, Android Studio also generates code for the read and reply intents and the messaging service, the details of which are covered in chapter 7. A real world Auto messaging app will typically use an Android service that connects to a back end system to facilitate communication.

We covered in this chapter, the steps entailed in extending an Android app's notifications into the Android Auto platform. The entire source code of the two application flavors that covered in this chapter is available as part of the source code for this book, under apps/0HelloAutoB and apps/0HelloAutoA.

References & Further Reading

http://developer.android.com/reference/android/app/AlarmManager.html
http://developer.android.com/reference/android/app/PendingIntent.html
http://developer.android.com/reference/android/app/NotificationManager.html
http://developer.android.com/reference/android/support/v4/app/NotificationCompat.html
https://www.google.com/design/spec-auto/designing-for-android-auto/design-principles.html
https://www.google.com/design/spec-auto/designing-for-android-auto/designing-for-cars.html
https://www.google.com/events/io/io14videos/6a888fa5-b7cf-e311-b297-00155d5066d7
https://source.android.com/devices/accessories/protocol.html
https://developers.google.com/android/reference/com/google/android/gms/location/FusedLocatio
nProviderApiAtt

For the purpose of reading the rest of this book, the use of a "real" *Android Auto* head-unit in your automobile is not essential. You may defer the procurement of your *Android Auto* head-unit until the time is right for you. The head-unit emulator(DHU) that we covered in earlier chapters is a high quality development tool that gives us a good sense of the in-vehicle user experience. Yet, the real-time and mobile nature of automobile transportation means that there remains much to be experienced and understood via driving a vehicle with a real *Android Auto* compatible head-unit in action – as a precursor to designing, developing, and releasing applications that you have extended to *Android Auto*.

If you currently happen to drive a recent automobile model (2015 onwards), it would be worthwhile to check if its head-unit happens to support *Android Auto*. Automobile head-units typically support a wide range of competing standards. In case you are considering purchasing a car in the near future – as an Android enthusiast, developer, and consumer– you may choose a model whose dashboard infotainment system supports *Android Auto* and also meets your various other criteria. Because *Android Auto* has widespread support from most major auto-manufacturers, it is unlikely that your choice of automobile will be constrained in any way. Alternatively, you may consider purchasing an after-market *Android Auto* compatible head unit for installation in your existing automobile.

Android Auto, after-market head-unit

Installing an after-market head-unit in your current vehicle is a quick and immediate – though not necessarily inexpensive – way to experience the *Android Auto* platform.

Procuring an after-market head-unit

As such, any after-market car infotainment system that clearly declares its support for and/or compatibility with "*Android Auto*" should work, at least in theory. It is relevant to mention here, that some head-unit/ car infotainment product listings contain terms such as "**Android based**" and that as it turns out is **not** the same as "***Android Auto***" compatible. The open source nature of Android makes it possible for a head-unit device maker to leverage the free and open source Android OS and build their custom flavor of the OS and use it on their devices and products. Android as a mobile phone operating system has relevance when run in the head-unit, only after making careful modifications that address safety and user experience design considerations.

Whether a head-unit's base operating system runs an Android derived OS is actually irrelevant when it comes to compatibility with *Android Auto*. There are several head-unit products available in the marketplace, that run or claim to run "Android", and many if not most of these are actually incompatible with *Android Auto*. What matters is whether the head-unit product catalog/listing clearly declares **support** for ***Android Auto*** (and includes under the covers, the implementation of the *Android Auto protocol* which enables the head-unit to serve as an projection system for the Android phone device). Also, the list of electronic manufacturers who support *Android Auto* is available at: http://www.openautoalliance.net/#members under "Technology Partners" at the bottom of the page. You should expect the manufacturer of an *Android Auto* compatible after-market head-unit model that you are considering purchasing, to be listed as a member of the *Open Automotive Alliance* and/or at https://www.android.com/auto/. The listed technology partners include electronics manufacturers such as JVC Kenwood, Panasonic, Pioneer, Parrot Automobile, LG, Denso, Symphony Teleca, and Magneti Marelli. Only particular after-market infotainment system models from these listed manufacturers support *Android Auto*. Also, not all such listed electronic makers have current products offerings in the after-market market segment though. Many product offerings from these makers are aimed exclusively at the OEM segment. In a dynamic market place, product offerings are ever evolving, so it is important to do your own research. You will find numerous *Android Auto* compatible head-unit models available at local car stereo stores and major on-line retailers with price tags that start at about US $400 upwards. Please be guided by the specification sheets, online reviews per your judgment, and the *Open Automotive Alliance* member listing in order to choose a suitable *Android Auto* head-unit. Google reportedly makes the *Android Auto protocol* implementation library – which makes it possible for a head-unit to support *Android Auto* – available to the *Open Automotive Alliance*. There is also expectedly some testing, validation, and certification steps that are performed. The *Android Auto protocol* implementation is is likely not covered by an open source license and its source code is not publicly available as far as I am aware. The finer points of Linux software licensing allow for the kernel to load self-contained proprietary modules.

I purchased the *Pioneer AVIC-8100NEX In-Dash Navigation System®* from *amazon.com* around mid 2015. This particular unit was one of many *Android Auto* compatible, after-market head-unit products that were available in the marketplace.

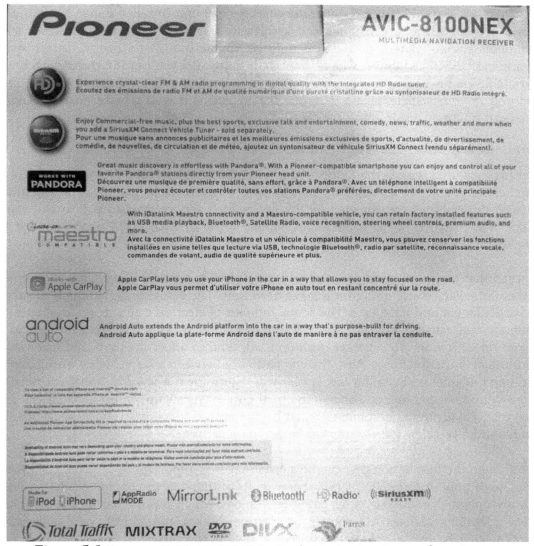

Figure **5-1** Pioneer AVIC-8100NEX In-Dash Navigation System® packaging

Figure 5-1 shows the packing box of the Pioneer head-unit that I purchased, with the term "**android auto**" prominently displayed (along with support for a multitude of other relevant automobile infotainment standards). The unequivocal declaration of support for *Android Auto* in the product's online catalog and a few apparently authentic online reviews gave me the assurance that the product I chose would serve my need for an *Android Auto* compatible head-unit. Although I was not disappointed after I had my original OEM head-unit taken out and the *Android Auto* after-market head-unit installed in my Toyota Camry Hybrid car -- both as a consumer and a software engineer, there were however a few automobile engine related features (car mileage, engine status, and hybrid battery status) the original OEM head-unit – which I replaced – provided via user interfaces, which were unavailable via the new after-market *Android Auto* head-unit. If you have an existing OEM head-unit in your vehicle, please be aware that replacing it with an after-market *Android Auto* head-unit may result in loss of access to particular engine related information.

Installation of after-market head-unit

After taking a brief look at the Pioneer head-unit's packing box content which included the main head unit and various adapters and cables, I sought the advice of my local automobile (Toyota) dealership. I was directed by the dealership's service department, to an external vendor who installed my new head-unit, replacing the original OEM head-unit that had come with the vehicle originally.

I learned that the installation cost can vary considerably, from $200 upwards and depends on the particular vehicle and after market head-unit. The actual price will tend to vary by the particular car and head-unit. The actual number of electronic controls related to audio, telephone and cameras that are available on your steering wheel, which will need to get hooked up with your after-market head-unit will tend to affect the parts and labor effort, and ultimately the total cost. Also, the compatibility between your vehicle's wiring and the head-unit's adapter and cabling accessories will determine if a few additional adapters and cables will be needed or not. For me, the total cost of installation approximated US $500. After that, I had my automobile checked by the auto dealership's service department to verify that the vehicle's main wiring was intact in every way.

Even though the installation cost can be substantial, it is important to seek the professional expertise of your automobile manufacturer or its authorized dealership. Modern vehicles typically operate via drive-by-wire based technology which means that under the covers, critical functions such as the control of steering, brakes and throttle, are achieved via electrical signals and electronic circuitry. Although the steering, throttle and braking interfaces that the driver operates are mechanical, these get converted into corresponding electrical signals. The core functions of the vehicle are achieved via wiring and circuitry that runs within narrow confines and it is critical that qualified service personnel access the vehicle wiring and install your after-market head-unit, in the interest of public safety and your individual safety.

After-market head-unit, first run

Once the after-market head-unit has been installed in your vehicle, you will find that it includes a USB connector for connecting your phone over USB. Your phone will naturally need to have the *Android Auto app* installed. It would be best to turn off *Android Auto developer mode*, as the *Head-unit server* (better named DHU server) has no relevance when connecting to a physical head-unit.

Your car should be parked and the parking brake applied, prior to – and during the process of – connecting your Android phone to the head-unit via the USB cable, the very first time. In case you fail to do so, you should expect to see a helpful relevant suggestion and you will need to start over. Once your phone and head-unit detect each other, you will need to accept the applicable safety and legal terms and conditions. The requirement that the vehicle be parked the first time, is a safety requirement that ensures that the driver is able to read the relevant safety and legal information and take the time to get familiar with the system's interfaces and behavior while parked.

Figure **5-2** Android phone – head-unit connection, first time steps

Figure 5-2 shows the screen that was displayed on my Android phone upon connecting it to my Pioneer head-unit, while my car was stopped but with the engine running, and the parking brake off. The message on the screen reads *"Android Auto will resume when your car's parked. Already parked? Engage the parking brake."* After turning off the ignition, engaging the parking brake, and then powering up the vehicle with the phone connected over USB, I was able to get my *Android Auto* system to engage – my phone displayed the *Android Auto* screen lock, while the head-unit displayed the "Home" screen.

The figure series 5-3, 5-4, 5-5, 5-6, and 5-7 show the first level screens for Map, Phone, Home, Music, and Native sections respectively.

Home

The Home screen is the initial screen that gets displayed and looks much like the DHU's home screen (Figure 5-3). As we covered earlier, the home screen typically includes timely and relevant suggestion cards for destination, music and weather information. It may also include information about a recent phone call or message.

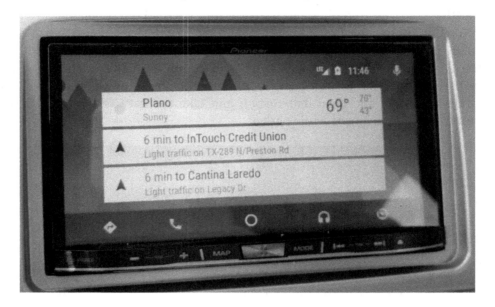

Figure **5-3** Home screen with suggestion cards, Pioneer AVIC-8100NEX after-market

Maps

Maps, navigation, and driving directions represent for most users the most important and used feature in the automobile infotainment system. As drivers many of us have come to rely on the driving destinations routinely, even for those destinations familiar to us – for availing of conveniences such as expected time of arrival, live traffic information, and detour recommendations to bypass traffic congestions

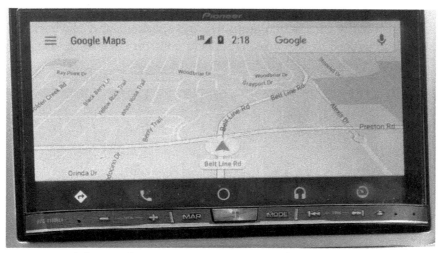

Figure **5-4** Google Maps app on Pioneer after-market head unit

Phone

Android Auto provides hands-free calling via tapping a contact in the touch screen, or tapping on the microphone icon displayed in the top right (or using the steering wheel's call button) and then speaking the name of the contact.

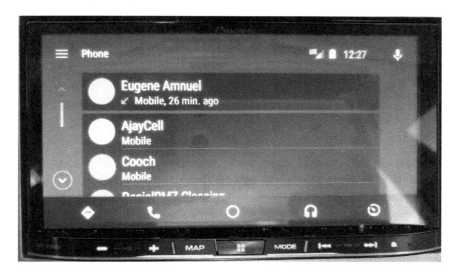

Figure **5-5** Phone, Pioneer AVIC-8100NEX after-market head-unit

Music

Music gets played via the car's stereo amplifier and speakers; and playback control works via the touch screen as well as the steering wheel's controls such as pause and skip to the next song.

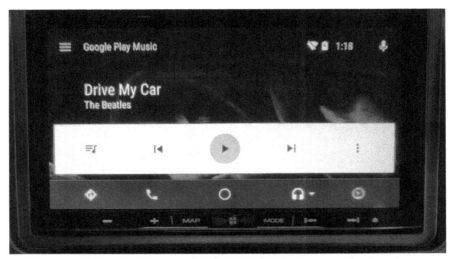

Figure **5-6** Music, Pioneer AVIC-8100NEX after-market head-unit

The real head-unit's visual interfaces are virtually identical to the Desktop Head Unit (DHU). There is however a difference in user experience while using the head-unit while actually driving your car, compared to the DHU. Maps for instance, displays the maps of your current location along with the directional pointer icon which changes on a live basis as the vehicle moves and changes direction. Also, the steering wheel functions pertinent to audio, voice, and phone are available as an alternative to using the head-unit's touch screen.

"Native interface"

Even when connected in *Android Auto mode*, you have the choice of accessing the native interface and its functionality, via accessing the *Return to <Native>* function – the gateway into the native non-Android Auto user experience in your car. You might recall from chapter 4, that the DHU/emulator displays, upon touching the "native access" action (at the bottom right of the main screen), the "***Return to Google***" menu which does nothing when tapped. On a real vehicle though, you get access to the entire set of native functions such as maps, music including radio and CD player, and phone, as available in the native head-unit – in this case the Pioneer head-unit. This allows you to access particular functions that are unavailable in *Android Auto.*

Figure **5-7** Native access, Pioneer AVIC-8100NEX after-market head-unit

Exploring the "native" Pioneer AVIC-8100NEX head-unit

The "native" Pioneer AVIX-8100NEX head-unit is a stand-alone entertainment system that can work independently, irrespective of *Android Auto.*

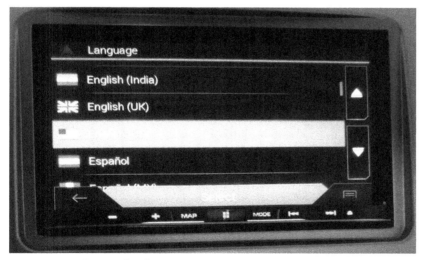

Figure **5-8A** First time setup, Pioneer AVIC-8100NEX

As covered in chapter 2, one of the advantages of *Android Auto* is that head-unit makers can build their own native features and user interfaces, while also supporting *Android Auto* and other standards and protocols. This gives consumers the choice of different platforms and associated user experience and interaction. The Pioneer head-unit includes features such as maps, radio, CD player, and phone integration over Bluetooth. Figures 5-8A through 5-8D show a few of the native screens and controls. The first time I accessed the native head unit, a few screens pertaining to first time setup popped up (Figure 5-8A). This category of preferences entry represents the one time overhead that a user must incur towards the setting up of language and preferences, when engaging with a new native infotainment system device.

Figure **5-8B** native System menu, Pioneer after-market head-unit

The native *System* settings (Figure 5-8B) includes various secondary settings that some consumers may find of interest. I had personally, previously been using the radio and CD player of my original OEM head-unit which had lacked items such as MIXTRAX and SiriusXM, and therefore I had no particular affinity towards them.

In the long run, it is certainly possible that the *Android Auto protocol* will expand its capabilities to address the syncing of preferences data from Google/Android into the native head-unit, with the user's approval – simply by first connecting to a new head-unit using *Android Auto*, the driver's basic preferences would get updated automatically, under the covers.

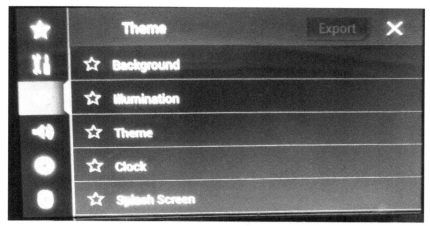

Figure **5-8C** native theme, Pioneer after-market head-unit

The native *Theme* setting allows you to customize the display properties. I let the default settings remain in place.

Figure **5-8D** maps, Pioneer after-market head-unit

Figure 5-D shows the native Pioneer head-unit's maps and navigation system. I personally found the Google Maps/*Android Auto* experience infinitely more compelling than the native map system and its user interactions. I discovered that when I switched from the *Android Auto* experience to the native experience while playing a song that was playing from my Google Music collection from the cloud, the Pioneer native player displayed the currently playing song and provided me playback controls (such as pause, stop etc.) as shown in Figure 5-8E.

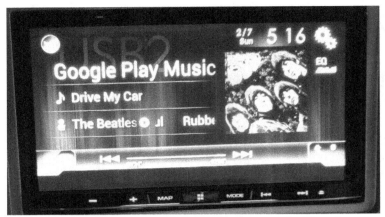

Figure **5-8E** Pioneer native music, after-market head-unit

On the other hand, if I commenced playing a song via the head-unit's CD player and subsequently switched into the *Android Auto* experience, *Android Auto* was unaware of the song that was playing on the CD player. It could be a defect in my head-unit's wiring, but it could instead very well be the expected behavior in that *Google Music* emphasizes cloud based music playback and probably does care about local media playback.

Figure **5-8E** Video setup

Many head-unit models including the Pioneer head-unit include DVD playback capability which feeds into screens that are positioned for viewing by passengers in the rear seats. The display of video content within the driver's range of vision is generally inconsistent with the best practices and/or applicable standards and regulations in most, if not all countries and regions.

Limitations of Android Auto w.r.t. "native" after-market head-unit

I found the *Android Auto* experience to be highly enjoyable, with negligible overhead of initial engagement and setup. The replacement of the original OEM head-unit that came with my car, with the after-market Pioneer head-unit, resulted in the loss of particular vehicle specific information such as the hybrid car's battery levels and mileage statistics. Due to the non-trivial overhead of time and cost of installation of the after-market unit, it is important to carefully weigh your options before deciding to remove your existing head-unit.

Android Auto OEM head-unit

The native OEM Android Auto enabled head-unit is one that comes preinstalled in the vehicle, and most consumers will end up experiencing *Android Auto* in this manner. In order to get a sense of the OEM experience, I test drove a Honda Accord and took a few photographs of the *Android Auto* experience.

Home

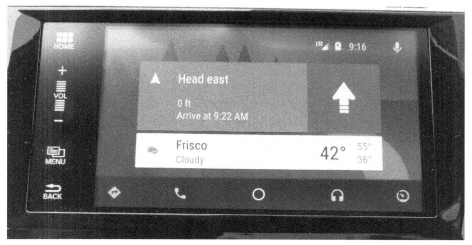

Figure 5-9A Home – Honda OEM head-unit

As expected, plugging in my Android phone into a vehicle's head-unit for the first time got me connected with the *Android Auto* experience with no overhead. The home screen of the OEM head-unit with a couple of suggestion cards (Figure 5-9A). The *Android Auto* navigation bar at the bottom was identical, while a few additional items such as *Home*, *Volume*, *Menu*, and *Back* were present on the left.

Maps

Figure 5-9B shows the *Google Maps* on the OEM head-unit screen and its look and feel was identical to that on my after-market head-unit. Phone and Music too — not shown in figures — were identical to that on after-market head-unit.

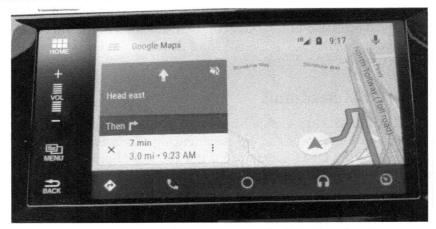

Figure **5-9B** Google Maps – Honda OEM head-unit

Native OEM interface

Although the *Android Auto* user experience on this OEM head-unit was indistinguishable from that on my Pioneer after-market head-unit unit, there was significant difference in the arena of the native interface. Compared to the after-market head-unit experience, the native OEM head-unit typically has the advantage of deeper integration with the automobile's engine status, metrics and statistics. This can include gas mileage or maintenance history and depends on the particular automobile manufacturer and model, though over time these nuggets of data may formally become available to the *Android Auto* platform.

Figure 5-10 shows the screen that provides access to the native OEM head-unit via the "Return to Honda" item shown but not adequately legible in the figure.

Figure **5-10**, accessing native OEM interface *"Return to Honda"*

Figure **5-11A**, native OEM interface, over view

Figure 5-11A shows the apps, settings and vehicle specific data access that are available on the Honda OEM head-unit. It also provides a menu item to go to *Android Auto* from the native user experience.

Native OEM vehicle fuel economy info

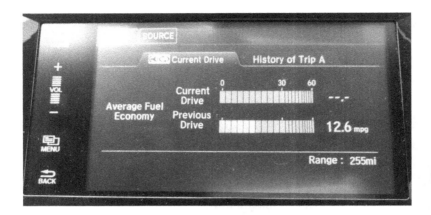

Figure **5-11B**, native OEM interface, fuel economy info

Figure 5-11B shows a native interface that displays the vehicle's fuel economy. The actual values are skewed on account of it being a brand new car.

Advantages of native OEM head-unit

While the native OEM interface is auto-manufacturer and model specific, some of the typical features and functions include vehicle specific information and integration with hardware such as vehicle mounted cameras for parking assistance and more. After-market head-units are currently incapable of providing such device information. In fact, the hope is that over time, the *Android Auto protocol* will expand its capabilities so that *Android Auto* can support deeper vehicle data and functional integration into the *Android Auto* platform.

Running apps on physical head-units during development

Now that we have covered the subject of the in-vehicle head-unit experience with regard to the basic *Android Auto* functionality, let us progress into the arena of running your own self developed apps on the in-vehicle head-unit rather than the DHU. As an experiment, I set the alarm in the Hello Auto(A) app which we covered in chapter 4 and then connected my phone to my vehicle's head-unit. The notification did not show up after 3 minutes. Due to technical, legal, and security reasons, this is the expected behavior – Google requires every *Android Auto* application to be formally signed, versioned and released via their Play Store even during development, before it can be executed via a vehicle's head-unit. When you stop to think about it for a few moments, you realize that running a development version of your *Android Auto* app on a **real** vehicle head-unit effectively makes it a

production app from the start.

Google Play Store, Play Developer Console, Alpha/Beta distribution

The Google *Play Store* app which is typically found pre-installed on Android devices sold in most countries worldwide, allows users to install other free or paid Android apps published and publicly available in the Google Play app distribution platform. The Google Play store was originally named "Android Market". While consumers use the Google Play Store app and web based platform (https://play.google.com/) to view the catalog of apps, books, music, and more, the app developers use the play console to publish apps (https://play.google.com/apps/publish).

Starting in 2013, Google's Play developer console added a feature that allowed developers to distribute early/work-in-progress **alpha/beta** versions of their apps privately to select users such as internal team members, clients, partners, and interested consumers. As such this private distribution channel is highly useful and convenient for internal distribution of work-in-progress apps. This approach gives users the experience that most closely resembles the real world life cycle app installation and updates. It also boosts security as users do not need to "weaken" their devices' security by allowing their devices to "install apps from unknown sources" via the Android device's Settings. Many development environments today leverage the Playstore's private Alpha/Beta distribution channel for internal, partner, and client distribution of early versions of apps. This engages product and engineering teams with the *Google Play Developer Console* and the app publisher catalog with description, graphics, target audience, legalities and more; it also helps explore the off-the-shelf statistics. Leveraging the Play Store platform early in alpha and beta is generally acknowledged as useful, effective, and relevant for any app that is intended for eventual public release.

Android Auto and Google Playstore, Alpha/Beta

While the use of the *Play Store* alpha/beta channel is optional to use for Android apps in general, in order to get your work-in-progress *Android **Auto*** app to get extended to a physical *Android Auto head-unit* in your automobile, it is essential to release the app via Google Playstore's Alpha/Beta channel. Due to driver safety and binary code security considerations, Google enforces the requirement that your development app be signed and released via the Alpha/Beta channel while in development before its execution can be extended into an automobile's head-unit. Google's *Android Auto App* plays a key role in the mechanism of your *Android Auto* application's extension into the head-unit – DHU or real – and therefore it is both responsible for enforcing, and in a position to enforce, the rules.

Android Auto – steps for Alpha/Beta distribution via Android Play Console

All Android apps need to be digitally signed in order to be installable on Android devices. During development, the build tools engage a debug certificate by default, in order to automatically sign your apps using this debug certificate. This debug keystore is typically located in a directory named ".android" under your user home directory. The keystore is a repository for digital certificates. The following listing displays the debug keystore's location on my development computer:

```
~ $ ls -lt /home/sanjay/.android/debug.keystore
-rw-rw-r-- 1 sanjay sanjay 2149 Oct 15 07:40 /home/sanjay/.android/debug.keystore
~ $
```

Whenever you distribute an app via the Play Store, be it in for production (public) or Alpha/Beta (private), you will need to use an apk that has been digitally signed with a release certificate; the debug certificate will not work for this purpose. This release certificate does not need to be signed by any certificate authority - it may be self-signed, by you. However the validity of the certificate must extend beyond 25 years hence. This release certificate is used by Google to uniquely identify the author of the app. More information on Android **App signing** is available at: http://developer.android.com/tools/publishing/app-signing.html.

Its very important to retain your keystore and associated credentials in a secure location and maintain adequate backups. It is also important to use strong keystore and alias passwords. After you publish an app to the Play Store, all subsequent versions of the app will need to be signed using the same keystore. If you should lose your release keystore after publishing your app to the Play Store, you will not be able to release any further update versions of your app. Moreover, if some third party gains access to your keystore and the password credentials (or can guess the passwords), they may possibly gain the ability to release updates that replace apps owned by you.

Creating a self signed keystore

This release keystore does not need to be created on a per app basis, though it can be a good practice to do so in some scenarios, for instance if you are an App developer who is building an app for your client or customer.

In order to distribute the *HelloAuto(A)* app to the Play Store, I ended up creating a separate keystore. More information on the keytool command can be found at: https://docs.oracle.com/javase/8/docs/technotes/tools/unix/keytool.html. I used the following command to create the keystore and made a note of its alias and the password that I entered, as indicated in the snippet below:

```
$ keytool -genkey -v -keystore helloAuto.keystore -alias
helloAuto -keyalg RSA -keysize 3072 -validity 50000
Enter keystore password: **********
```

I modified the *app/build.gradle* file per the directions in the **App signing** link reference above and build the release version of the apk.

```
2helloAutoA_prod $ ls -lt app/build/outputs/apk/
-rw-rw-r-- 1 sanjay sanjay 1434491 Nov 30 11:44 2_helloAutoA_1.0-release.apk
-rw-rw-r-- 1 sanjay sanjay 1434141 Nov 30 11:44 2_helloAutoA_1.0-release-unaligned.apk
```

I un-installed the earlier debug version of the *HelloAuto(A)* app before installing, running and verifying the functioning of this app on my Android device and the DHU. Next, I un-installed this app again, as the next steps entail distributing this app via the Play Store Alpha/Beta channel.

Google Play Developer Console Listing

I logged into the *Google Play Developer Console* at : https://play.google.com/apps/publish and attempted to "Add a new Application". Attempting to upload the apk failed with the error message:

> "Upload failed
> You must accept the Android Auto Addendum before uploading an Android Auto-enabled APK. You can do this from the Pricing and Distribution page."

Figure 5-12 shows the screenshot of the Upload failure message. General information about the *Android Auto addendum* is available at: https://play.google.com/about/auto/developer-distribution-agreement-addendum.html. I proceeded to the **Pricing and Distribution** section in order to locate the *Android Auto addendum*.

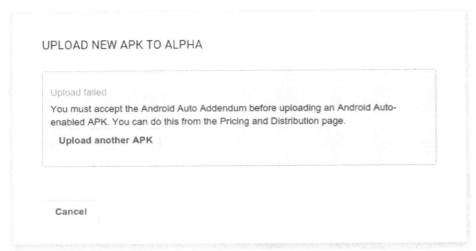

Figure **5-12** Upload failure / Android Auto addendum acceptance required

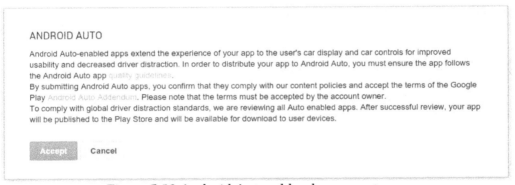

Figure **5-13** Android Auto addendum acceptance

Figure 5-13 shows the *Android Auto addendum* which I accepted after reading through the details. The contents of the terms – which may undergo revision from time to time – are reproduced in the snippet below:

ANDROID AUTO

Android Auto-enabled apps extend the experience of your app to the user's car display and car controls for improved usability and decreased driver distraction. In order to distribute your app to Android Auto, you must ensure that the app follows the Android Auto app **quality guidelines**.

By submitting Android Auto apps, you confirm that they comply with out content policies and accept the terms of the Google Play Android Auto Addendum. Please note that the terms must be accepted by the account owner. To comply with globarl driver distraction standards, we are reviewing all Auto enabled apps. After successful review, your app will be published to the Play Store and will be available for download to user devices.

Android Auto app quality guidelines are available at: http://developer.android.com/distribute/essentials/quality/auto.html. I proceed to provide all the relevant information, under the various headings of *APK, Content and Rating, Pricing and Distribution*. I limited the target countries to the United States as that is where I reside. I could recommend that initially, it is useful to limit the target countries to as small a set as possible. That's because country specific laws are applicable to in-vehicle infotainment systems and the matters of driver distraction and associated standards. Limiting the number of countries that your Auto app is targeted to initially, will tend to reduce the volume of requirements that your application will need to satisfy initially. It will be more manageable to get approved for one target country before incrementally expanding out.

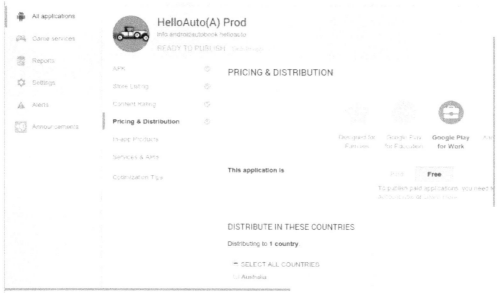

Figure **5-14** Play Store - ready to publish

I submitted this app for approval and received an email response (from <u>android-auto-review@gmail.com</u>) within a few hours indicating that the app had not been accepted. The snippet below shows some of the details:

```
"...
App status: Your app has not been accepted into Android Auto, and the
update is not live on Google Play.
Version Name: 1.0
Version Code: 1
Production Track: ALPHA
Rejection reasons:
- At this time, we are only accepting apps within the Media or short
form Messaging categories for Android Auto. Media apps that use TTS
engine readout for content are not permitted at this time.
Next Steps:
1. Make the necessary changes to your app.
2. Submit your app for another review.
Or, if you'd like to exclude your app from Android Auto:
1. Remove the Android Auto manifest entry from your APK code.
2. Sign in to your Developer Console and upload the new APK.
..."
```

I responded to the email from *android-auto-review* by emphasizing that my app was merely extending a one time, simple short text message to *Android Auto*, and not implementing any "TTS readout for content"; in fact the "TTS readout of content" was a behavior that the *Android Auto* platform, rather than my app was introducing. After several exchanges and explanations from my side, I did not get a specific answer. I had got nowhere in my endeavor to get my simple messaging app released in private closed alpha. This app's user experience was identical to that of an inbound text message via Google's Hangout app on *Android Auto*.

As I struggled while attempting to release the *HelloAuto(A)* app via the Google Play store during the last quarter of year 2015, I got the impression that Google was still in the process of firming up their internal guidelines for the approval of *Android Auto* apps and was more restrictive in the very early days of *Android Auto* apps. I may revisit this matter later and if I do make any progress, I will be sure to update relevant notes into the online source code repo.

This experience that I am sharing with you Gentle Reader, actually does serve an important purpose — it emphasizes the reality that in sharp contrast to the rest of the Android app ecosystem, Android apps that you attempt to extend to *Android Auto* are highly regulated and subject to a review and approval process. If you are considering enabling your app for

Android Auto, it will behoove you to implement a small, discrete and minimal feature set and engage with the Play store and test the waters of the approval process as early as possible.

In this chapter, we covered the in-vehicle Android Auto experience, as well as the hands on steps of engaging with Google Play Store's approval process for getting your Android Auto enabled apps on to your own vehicle head-unit during development. Awareness about and engagement with this Android Auto approval process is especially relevant for experienced Android developers, as we have gotten accustomed to the zero barrier process that has been in place for Android mobile (non-Auto enabled) apps.

References and further reading

https://www.android.com/auto/
http://www.pioneerelectronics.com/PUSA/Car/NEX/AVIC-8100NEX
http://www.amazon.com/Pioneer-AVIC-8100NEX-Navigation-Capacitive-Touchscreen/dp/B00SKJHIY4
http://developer.android.com/tools/publishing/app-signing.html
https://en.wikipedia.org/wiki/Certificate_authority

Part III   DESIGN STANDARDS

This section provides an overview of the user interface and interactive design principles that influence the in-vehicle user experience. The *Android Auto* platform has specific design standards that are enforced during the Playstore review and release process.

CHAPTER 6   Design Principles, Play Store Requirements

Many consumer applications engage with their users via multiple "channels" – device form factors and user agents such as desktops, laptops, televisions, game consoles, mobile phones, tablets, smartwatches, and automobile head-units. The device form factor refers to the physical characteristics of the device, including shape, dimensions, weight, screen size, physical buttons, I/O peripherals, and layout, as well as its capabilities. The user agent refers to the client software via which the users engage with the platform. Chapter 1 of this book covered the topic of consumer – computing device interactions in a multi- device world. This chapter begins with a continuation of that discussion, as a precursor to covering the design principles to *Android Auto*.

Device form factor specific application flavors

Web sites, email, chat, and web applications represented the Internet revolution of the 1990s. There were many browsers (user agents) at that time, but the desktop computer represented the sole device form factor for practically all consumers. In recent years, as more websites began to be accessed via mobile phones, there was a rush to ensure that "mobile versions" of the websites were built, with an emphasis on reduced payload, and better viewing via mobile devices. In more recent years, smartphone platforms came into existence and new genres of mobile applications arrived to the consumer market place that offered a rich and engaging user experience that was close to the user and the user's context. Mobile phone applications have now commenced to engage with smartwatches, televisions, and the automobile.

In general, the design principles for any consumer application are a function of the device form factor, and its capabilities and constraints if any. Many an application or platform today offers its functions via various device form factors and corresponding variations of its user interfaces and interaction behaviors. The intricacies of the user experience are a function of many factors including the available real estate on the screen for that device form factor and the capabilities and constraints of the platform running the device. Additionally, the context of what the user is doing and where the user is expected to be while interacting with the device governs the user interaction and application behavior. It is therefore expected that there will be variations of the user experience and interaction on the different flavors of the application that are targeted to different device form factors, although the fundamental functions remain the same (eg. consume message, reply message – in the case of a messaging application).

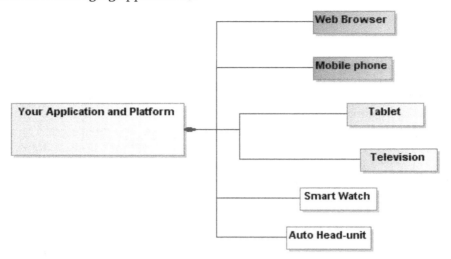

Figure **6-1** Application's device specific interaction flavors

Figure 6-1 shows an application/ platform that has a presence on a multitude of channels – browser, phone, tablet, television, smartwatch and automobile head-unit. Many applications may start out with an emphasis on one particular channel or the other and end up expanding into other relevant channels. Many applications will not ever be relevant for expansion or targeting to a particular device form factor. As a platform and application developer, you will need to periodically review and determine the set of device form factors that your platform has relevance for being targeted to.

Device form factor and coefficient of immersiveness

The coefficient of immersiveness of human attention refers to the degree of human attention that a given device form factor (and its applications and screen display content) can be expected to take up. The television for instance represents a device that has a relatively large screen size and is expected to reside within a consumer's living space and serve as a dedicated media consumption and entertainment device. Application user interfaces and content that are displayed on the television are expected to take up the user's attention completely and dedicatedly for time durations that could run into several hours, such as the time taken to watch a movie. A smartwatch on the other hand is expected to be worn on the user's wrist while engaged in a variety of daily activities. The watch based interactions are expected to be short lived and glance-able, the time duration of interactions are not expected to exceed very few seconds.

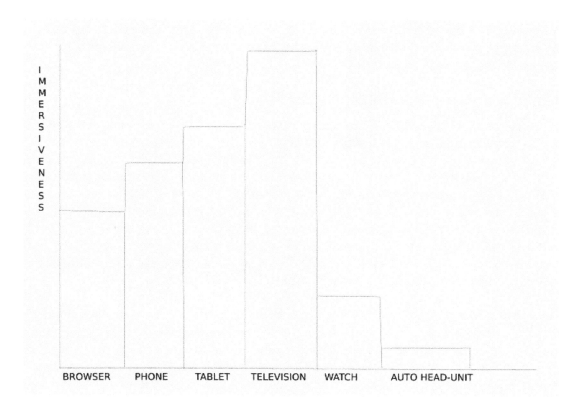

Figure **6-2** Co-efficient of impressiveness by user interaction channel

Figure 6-2 shows a general indicative estimation of how the coefficient of immersiveness of user attention might vary on an average, across standard device form factors and user agents. I have assumed that users tend to engage with their mobile smartphone apps to a greater degree than their the browser on the desktop or mobile device. Although many users use their phones more than their tablet, the engagement with the tablet often occurs in a setting when users have more time on their hands and are less on the move. In order to read a book or watch a video, you would likely choose a tablet if available to you at that time. The smartwatch though worn on the wrist for long durations, is typically used to read status updates and respond with brief messages via glance-able interactions. The television interaction on the other hand, often represents a more deeply immersive experience, such as watching a sporting event or a movie. While a given user might interact with the browser, phone, tablet, and smartwatch under a diverse range of circumstances and real world contexts, the automobile head-unit is unique in that the context and circumstance is strictly unvarying – the users are engaged in the rather serious activity of driving their automobile, and expected to keep their eyes on the road. Therefore, the head-unit's co-efficient of immersiveness is required to be as low as possible, and expected to be strictly enforced by the automobile head-unit platform.

Expanding your platform to *Android Auto*

As we have seen so far, the *Android Auto* platform currently supports maps and directions, phone and messaging, and music and audio playback. These represent the functions that are relevant to and supportive of the primary activity of driving safely. While maps and driving directions are intrinsic to driving, drivers often need information related to their destination and the party they are driving to meet. In the example of a parent driving to pick up a child, the exact time and location may need to get refined at the last moment and therefore access to updates via in-vehicle messaging and/or phone has much significance. It is thus inevitable that drivers end up needing access to basic hands-free messaging and phone functions. Audio playback has historically been available to drivers, and is generally considered to be complementary to driving safely.

While maps and driving directions, phone and messaging, and music and audio are available in the *Android Auto* head-unit, support for extending Android app functions are limited to a subset of the possibilities namely -- messaging and audio. Particularly application support for maps and driving directions as well as phone dialing functions are excluded from the scope of application functions that can be extended to *Android Auto*. At least, such is the case for the initial version of the *Android Auto* platform.

The *Android Auto* platform, via limiting its support for application functions to messaging and music/audio, is aligned with the principle of minimalism. It would certainly not be relevant for the vast majority of apps to be enabled for *Android Auto*, as firstly the functions of messaging and audio are present in a small subset of apps and secondly, not all messaging or audio functions in any given app would be relevant to the consumer while they are driving. Yet, it behooves app developers to become deeply aware of the *Android Auto* platform and its capabilities in order to explore the potential for strategically extending app(s) into *Android Auto*. Because both your app and the *Android Auto* platform will tend to evolve over time, it would be prudent to periodically review the latest *Android Auto* platform capabilities and evaluate whether the latest road map of your app has relevance for extension into the most current – and the emerging – definition of the *Android Auto*.

Android Auto - principles, standards and constraints

Within the backdrop of application support for the discrete and limited functions of messaging and audio that may be extended to *Android Auto*, there are many restrictions on the implementation of your *Android Auto* application, in terms of the interaction design, display characteristics, and application behavior. While Google publishes "suggestive" design guidelines for Android apps in general, Google's published standards for *Android Auto* are mandatory – apps that are enabled for *Android Auto* will need to adhere strictly to the principles such as minimization of user distraction, limitation of content, and subtle matters of contrast and visibility of information under varying light conditions.

Given this backdrop, even before you think of what app function you might extend to *Android Auto*, it is important to become deeply aware of the design guidelines, standards and principles for *Android Auto*. Not doing so, in a rush towards implementation without adequate familiarization of the platform and its standards and principles, can prove to be a futile and frustrating experience.

Design Principles for *Android Auto* apps

The *Android Auto* design principles are based on the prominent driving safety and distraction guidelines from all over the world. *Android Auto* apps are required to adhere to the design principles of simplicity, minimalism, content limitation, ease of readability, and glance-able interactions that are short lived and predictable – as described in detail at:
https://www.google.com/design/spec-auto/designing-for-android-auto/designing-for-cars.html
https://www.google.com/design/spec-auto/designing-for-android-auto/design-principles.html

It is important to refer to these and other resources made available by Google in order to stay current on the design principles for *Android Auto*. The rest of this section provides a brief summarization of these design principles.

Customization

It is important to customize the user interaction and screens specifically for the *Android Auto* platform, rather than attempt to transfer application functions from the mobile to the phone without all necessary adjustments.

Glanceable interactions

In order to minimize the distraction, it important for application screens to display minimal content that is easy to read – via a quick glance. Application screens should never require the driver's focused attention. Similarly the amount of information displayed will need to be limited.

What needs to be absolutely avoided

Animated images and video playback for instance are typically not allowed per the safety standards. Login and account sign up are functions that can be performed via the phone and are best kept out of the head-unit interaction. The following functions need to be absolutely avoided:

    account sign up
    login
    preferences and settings
    video playback
    animated images
    advertisements

Typography, fonts and sizing

Android Auto uses the **Roboto** font for consistency with phone and tablet devices. The platform leverages two discrete font sizes for ease of readability across head-unit displays. The primary font size should be used for items that need driver input such as a destination location or a song to play. The secondary, smaller font size should be used for supplemental information such as the estimated arrival time for the driving destination or the artist's name for a song. More information can be found at : https://www.google.com/design/spec-auto/designing-for-android-auto/minimizing-driver-distraction.html#minimizing-driver-distraction-typography.

Colors and contrast

The standards require sufficient contrast between the foreground (text and icons) and the background (color, album art, artist images) that accommodates all ambient lighting conditions including shade, direct sunlight, as well as night time and day time.

Day and Night modes

Night time interfaces are required to have light text with a dark background, while day time interfaces may have dark text on a light background or light text on a darker background. Figures 6-3A and 6-3B show the *Google Play Music app* in day and night modes respectively as an example.

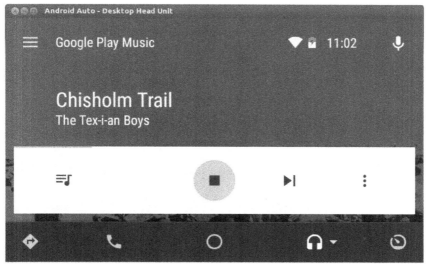

Figure **6-3A** Light text, darker background in day mode (Google Play Music)

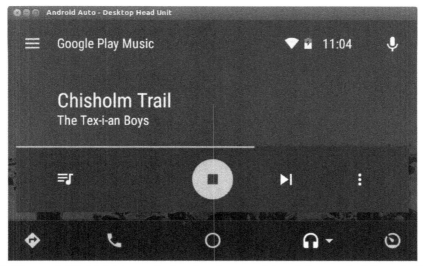

Figure **6-3B** Figure 6-3B Light text, darker background in night mode (Google Play Music)

Tap limit, tap tracking, runtime enforcements

Because the application's displayed content such as a list of songs may be received from cloud based end points, the application review process alone is not adequate for the *Android Auto* platform to enforce standards pertinent to limiting the amount of displayed content. The Android runtime monitors the number of taps that application interactions entail, and limits the number of taps for any interaction to 6 (in the United States) steps or taps. The tap limit may vary by country and locale. When the user accesses the navigation drawer by tapping, the system's counting for that user action commences. Scrolling to the next set of items in the list via a tap on the downward arrow, counts towards the maximum tap limit. Upon reaching the limit, further scrolling is prohibited and the system displays a suitable message and an icon, as seen at the bottom of the screen capture (Figure 6-4).

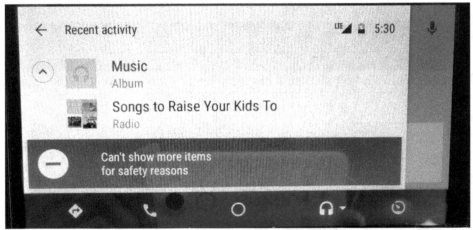

Figure **6-4** Tap limit enforcement

Android Auto app quality criteria

The quality criteria for *Android Auto* goes hand in hand with the design criteria covered in the earlier section and is well documented at: http://developer.android.com/distribute/essentials/quality/auto.html.

Figure 6-5 reproduces from the Android developer site, a tabulated summarization of these quality criteria. It includes test types such as Driver Attention, Layout Visual Contrast, and Interaction, and Tests or Test Codes such as AU-MV, AU-VA, and so on. Many of these criteria are fairly objective and straightforward. All the enumerated criteria represent the desired characteristics.

Type	Test	Description
Driver Attention	AU-MV	App does not display on the Auto screen animated elements such as animated graphics, video, or progress bars.
	AU-VA	App does not display any form of visual or text advertising on the Auto screen. Only audio ads are acceptable.
	AU-IM	App elements do not display any images on the Auto screen. Exceptions include: app may display a single static image for content context in the background of the consumption screen, such as album art, and app may display icons in the content navigation drawer.
	AU-DS	App does not include games or other features outside of the intended app types supported by Auto. (Learn How)
	AU-VI	App never activates the phone screen to present any form of visual information (notifications, toasts, video, images, advertising, etc.) on the phone screen while the app is interacting with the Android Auto dashboard unit.
Layout	AU-SC	App does not display automatically scrolling text.
Visual Contrast	AU-DM	App supports day mode, which renders dark text and controls on a light background. (Learn How)
	AU-NM	App supports night mode, which renders light text and controls on a dark background. (Learn How)
	AU-WI	App provides white icon sets that the system colorizes to provide automatic contrast compensation. (Learn How)
	AU-OC	App provides colors that the system can optimize for easy in-vehicle readability. (Learn How)
Interaction	AU-VC	App must support voice commands in audio apps. (Learn How)
	AU-AB	App-specific buttons respond to user actions with no more than a two-second delay.

Attribution : Android developer documentation
http://developer.android.com/distribute/essentials/quality/auto.html
Figure **6-5** Android Auto , app quality criteria, visual design & driver interaction

Anytime Google rejects a version of your Android Auto enabled app, one would expect that they will also provide the particular heading of test codes or code that was not met by your app, such as AU-SC which pertains to automatically scrolling text.

Android Auto approval process

In the previous chapter, we covered the hands on steps of distributing (or attempting to distribute) an application that has been extended to *Android Auto. Android Auto* enabled apps will need to be individually qualified and approved by Google. Unlike Android apps in general, which can be released to the Google Play Store without undergoing a review process, *Android Auto* Apps are required to be submitted for review before they can be approved for running on a real head-unit. The serious nature of driving makes it such that attempting to install an *Android Auto* application during development in private alpha or beta to your own automobile requires you to engage with a formal process, that appears at the time of writing to be as stringent as a formal production/ public market release. Once you get past the initial approval in alpha/beta, I anticipate that the same app can be tested internally in private alpha/beta and then released without additional steps. It is thus so very important to engage with the process at the earliest in order to limit the magnitude of surprises. The reference on *Play Store* distribution and approval is available at:
 http://developer.android.com/distribute/googleplay/auto.html.

Good luck !

This chapter provided an overview of the design principles pertinent to Android Auto applications that endeavors to complement Google's well documented design guidelines.

References and Further Reading

https://www.google.com/design/spec-auto/designing-for-android-auto/designing-for-cars.html
https://www.google.com/design/spec-auto/designing-for-android-auto/design-principles.html
https://www.google.com/design/spec-auto/designing-for-android-auto/minimizing-driver-distraction.html
https://developer.android.com/distribute/googleplay/auto.html
https://www.youtube.com/watch?v=vG9c5egwEYY
http://developer.android.com/tools/publishing/app-signing.html

Part IV   MESSAGING & AUDIO APIs

This section covers the messaging and audio related APIs pertinent to extending application functions to the *Android Auto* platform.

Any Android app that has been enabled for *Android Auto* messaging has the ability to extend its notifications into the head-unit's screen and allow the user to listen to messages and respond via voice input. The Hello Auto(A) app which was covered in chapter 4, is an instance of an *Android Auto* messaging app. This chapter covers in greater detail, the APIs that are relevant to extending messaging functions into the *Android Auto* platform. If your existing app implements some form of messaging, you may evaluate it for extension to *Android Auto*, if it has relevance for users while they are driving and does not introduce distraction.

Android Notifications

Android notifications represent a mechanism via which any Android app – even when it's not currently running in the foreground – can originate a short message that is intended to inform the user that some new information has arrived, or some event has occurred. The notification indicator icon shows up on the phone's global notification area in the status bar at the top left, and the details of the notification can be expanded via the notification drawer. Notifications are inherently associated with the user and the device, and operate at at a system level outside of the app. The Android system – rather than the app – manages notifications, the notification bar and the notification drawer. In order to write an *Android Auto* messaging app, you must leverage Android notifications and its extensions for *Android Auto*.

Suggest paradigm

Notifications are aligned with the "suggest" paradigm of human – computer interaction, in which the computing system endeavors to make timely and relevant recommendations and suggestions based on the user's current context (activity, location, destination, time of the day, calendar appointments and so on). The "demand" model which has been the traditional and long standing paradigm of human – computer interaction is somewhat on the decline today, as the recommendations, suggestions, predictions and personal agent oriented "suggest" model has gained prominence and significance. As timely and relevant recommendations and suggestions are presented to the user in real-time by intelligent agent algorithms, the user often does not need to ask for (ie. "demand") the obvious. Many of us have likely seen our phones display a notification that provides access to the relevant flight boarding pass upon arriving at an airport to catch a flight, or convenient access to providing a public review and rating for some retail location right after transacting some business there. As the intelligent agent based algorithms improve in their sophistication, we have seen in recent times, an increasing segment of user – computer interaction occurring via the "suggest" model. There is a theoretical limit to the "suggest" model though as all matters cannot always be suggested, at the right time and place, for all users. The suggest model thus co-exists with and complements the well established "demand" model.

Android 6 Notifications

Since Android notifications were introduced (nominally) in Android 3, they have undergone major upgrades in the many subsequent releases of the Android platform – versions 4, 5, and 6. Today, notifications have an increasingly significant role in application and interaction design, along with the increasing relevance of the suggest paradigm. Android 6 adds several new features to notifications such as the ability of an app to access the count of its currently active notifications and also the "reminder" category for notifications, which is distinct from the event and alarm categories of user scheduled items as detailed in the following section.

New Notification category "Reminder"

There are several category constants associated with notifications and these represent associated real world scenarios such as event, reminder, alarm, recommendation, email, call, message, system, and more. A system notification such as a low battery charge level also typically provides the user the means to turn on battery save mode.

Notification categories are useful for filtering which notifications can get to a user at a given time. There are times when the user is busy and sets their desired interruption levels via the settings which allows downtime and do-not-disturb time windows. Some notification categories such as an inbound phone call or message, a system notification such the "battery low" or a recommendation can occur at any unpredictable time. On the other hand, the user's calendar event, alarm or reminder (which can also cause notifications to originate) are typically set or scheduled by the user in advance. As a user, you may have several events and reminders in your calendar for a given day. An event typically has an associated time, a location and typically other participants. A "reminder" can be useful for encapsulating some human activity, task, to-do item or errand that the user needs to address in a given window of time. Reminders work well for encapsulating activities that have a weaker association with an exact time, place, and person(s), as in "buy eggs on the way home" or "call to wish grandma happy birthday, today". A lunch appointment or a scheduled conference call are better encapsulated as events as these have a specific time, participants, and/or location. The notifications associated with some instances of "reminders" potentially have relevance for *Android Auto* and driving – particularly the ones that pertain to picking up or dropping off someone or something. More details on the "reminder" category of notification can be found at:

http://developer.android.com/reference/android/app/Notification.html#CATEGORY_REMINDER

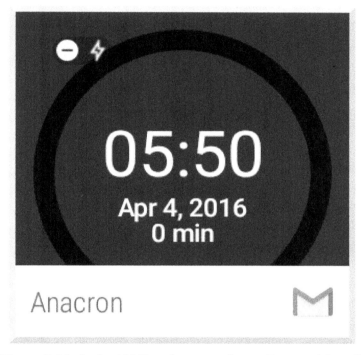

Figure **7-1A** Android Wear device with notification (Gmail)

Figure 7-1A shows a new email notification from Gmail, extended into an Android Wear smart watch device.

Figure 7-1B shows the numerous notifications that show up on my phone – the screen is full of notifications that are seen after expanding the notification drawer on the top left of the device. The next version of Android namely Android "N"/Android 7 which is in preview mode at the time of finishing up this book, has introduced new features such as *Direct reply* which allows users to respond quickly to brief communications from within the notification interface itself, and bundled notifications wherein the Android system has the ability to group related notifications together. As notifications have gained much prominence in recent years, the increasing number of notifications will benefit from bundled notifications.

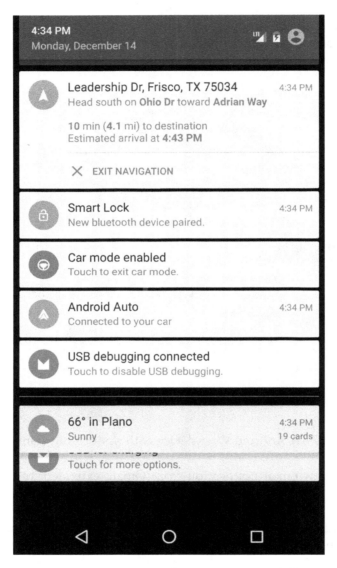

Figure **7-1B** Notifications - screen full

Figure **7-1C** Android Wear smartwatch - incoming call notification

Figure 7-1C shows a notification that was extended to my Android Wear smart watch, from the Android phone dialer app executing on my phone.

NotificationManager

Android's *NotificationManager* is one of several system services. The Android OS implements and executes a multitude of system services such as activity manager, package manager, audio manager, power manager, notification manager, etc. These services execute in the *system_server* process and are available to application code via service objects that are bound to the corresponding running service implementations. Such service objects are not instantiated directly, rather they are looked up by name by the application components via invocation of the *Context.getSystemService* method with the appropriate argument.

The handle to the service is strongly associated with the particular Activity, Service, or Provider's context via which it was originally obtained, and is not recommended for being passed between components. Since all components have access to their context — needed for calling *getSystemServices* — there is little to be gained by attempting to cache or share the service handle across components within an application.

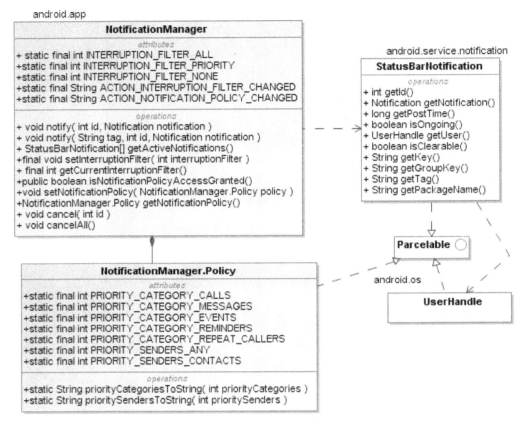

Figure **7-2** NotificationManager, StatusBarNotification classes partial listing

Figure 7-2 shows some of the attributes and methods in the *NotificationManager* and *StatusBarNotification* classes. The *NotificationManager*'s *notify()* method is used for originating a notification. The *id* used to originate the notification should be unique within the application, when used without the tag in the *notify()* method. When the overloaded *notify (tag, id,...)* is used, the tag-id pair must be unique within your application.

StatusBarNotification

StatusBarNotification which was introduced in API level 18, represents a data structure that encapsulates the notification that's displayed on the status bar. The *StatusBarNotification* class has getter methods for accessing its numerous attributes such as the encapsulated notification, the time the notification was posted and whether the notification is ongoing. An ongoing notification is associated with the flag *FLAG_ONGOING_EVENT* which is a static constant in the *Notification* class and useful for representing events that span a duration of time such as an ongoing phone call, a USB debugging session, or a running *Android Auto Head-unit server*.

Other notifications such as a missed call or an email that has arrived, are instantaneous and not ongoing by nature, therefore they do not benefit from setting the ongoing attribute.

PendingIntent

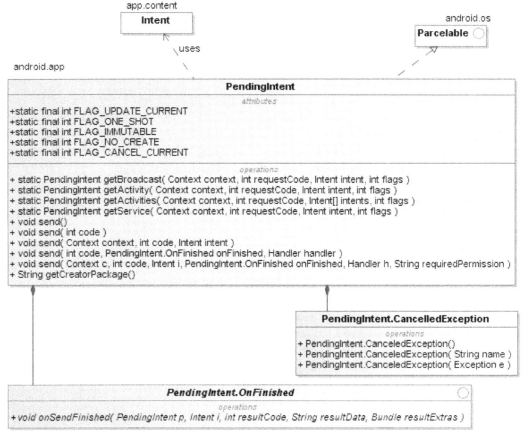

Figure **7-3** PendingIntent class diagram, partial listing

The *Intent* is a data structure that represents an action or operation that needs to be performed; it is intercepted and handled by the Android platform at runtime and serves as a late binding mechanism that allows one component to start another component – within the same application or within a different application. The Intent class resides in the package *android.content*.

The *PendingIntent* resides in the package *android.app* and is similar to – but not directly hierarchically associated with – the *Intent*. The *PendingIntent* defines an action that one application can get another application to perform in its behalf. The security permission constraints of the original app are applied to the execution of the operation by the Android runtime. Figure 7-3 shows the *PendingIntent* class and some of its methods and attributes. An instance of *PendingIntent* can be obtained via calling one of its static *getActivity*, *getService* or *getBroadcast* methods and corresponding to these the obtained pending intent will be associated with the starting an activity, the starting a service or the originating a broadcast. The overloaded *getActivity()* family of methods include several variants, not shown in the class diagram. Also not shown in the diagram are the variants of the overloaded *getActivities* family of methods. The overloaded *send()* method pertains to execution of the operation that the pending intent encapsulates. The static final FLAG_* family of attributes help specify the finer points of the pending intent's behavior such as whether a given intent is to be immutable or update-able. The static *PendingIntent.OnFinished* interface has the *onSendFinished()* method which enables application code to discover when the send operation finished. More details about *PendingIntent* can be found at:

http://developer.android.com/reference/android/app/PendingIntent.html.

RemoteInput

If your notification has an associated action for receiving simple text input, that is easy enough to accomplish on a phone or tablet (hand-held) device via application user interfaces and keyboard (or voice input to the hand-held device that the app is running on). In case of notifications that have been extended to *Android Wear* or *Android Auto* – which are platforms which emphasize voice input and have limitations or constraints with respect to keyboard input – the remote input mechanism that is associated with the notification action can receive voice input into the platform extension device and make it available as a string in the main application that's running in the hand-held device.

A *RemoteInput* object enables platform extensions to *Android Wear* and *Android Auto* (for which the keyboard is lacking or inappropriate) to receive voice input and then make it available as string input to the application that's running on the hand-held device. Such remote input may be free form as in a dictated text message, or choice based discrete options, such as "Yes" or "No".

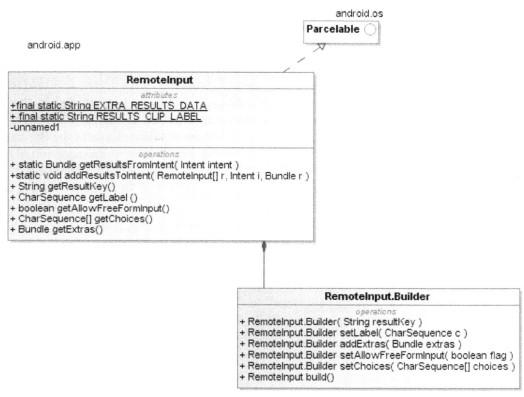

Figure **7-4** RemoteInput class diagram, partial listing

The extended (Wear or Auto) platform device serves as a remote input device with respect to the hand-held device, on which the main application is executing. Figure 7-4 shows the *RemoteInput* class whose static inner *RemoteInput.Builder* facilitates building an instance of *RemoteInput*. The builder's constructor requires a key string that represents an action. The *setLabel* method facilitates setting the human readable label to be displayed when soliciting voice input. The following pseudo code snippet shows the instantiation of a *RemoteInput* object :

```
RemoteInput remoteInput =
    new RemoteInput.Builder (YOUR_APP_EXTRA)
        .setLabel ("your App label")
        .build();
```

In the next version of Android – Android "N" / Android 7 – it expected that the remote input mechanism will enable users to reply to incoming notifications without leaving the notification using the Direct Reply feature:

http://developer.android.com/preview/features/notification-updates.html

Extending Notifications to Android Auto

Extending notifications to *Android Auto* entails working with *NotificationManager*, *CarExtender*, *PendingIntent*, and *RemoteInput*. The *CarExtender* is included in the core API for Android version 6 and onward and is similar in function to the *WearableExtender*, which facilitates extending an Android app to the *Android Wear* platform. In the case of *Android Wear*, an app can engage with *Android Wear* not only via remote input but also via creating a Wear flavor of the app that will actually execute on the *Android Wear* device and this represents a deeper degree of engagement than remote input. In case of *Android Auto*, the option of building an app that executes primarily on an *Android Auto* compatible head-unit does not exist at this time (as mentioned earlier in this book). Therefore extension of messaging function into the automobile head-unit must occur with the *CarExtender*. The static inner class *CarExtender* which is available in *android.app.Notification* is the key to extending notifications into the *Android Auto* platform.

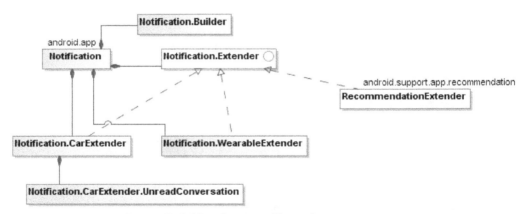

Figure **7-5** *Notification, Extender*s overview

Figure 7-5 shows the overview of the *Notification* class and the *Extender* interface and its implementing classes. The *Notification* contains the static inner *Extender* interface as well as static inner classes *CarExtender* and *WearableExtender,* both of which implement the static inner *Extender* interface. The *extend(Notification.Extender)* method available in the *Notification.Builder* facilitates extending a notification into *Android Auto* (as well as Android Wear).

NotificationManager.CarExtender

Notification.CarExtender.Builder provides methods that facilitate adding messages and setting the read pending intent and the reply action. The *build()* method of *Notification.CarExtender.Builder* builds an instance – not of the *CarExtender* but – of the *UnreadConversation*. The *UnreadConversation* in turn may have one or more messages depending on the number of *addMessage* calls that were invoked on the *Notification.CarExtender.Builder*.

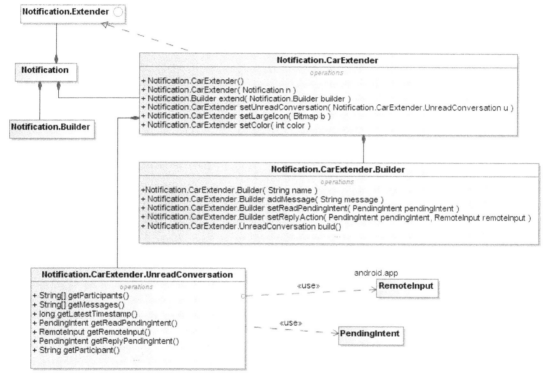

Figure **7-6** CarExtender, UnreadConversation, class diagram, partial listing

Figure 7-6 shows details of the *Notification.CarExtender* and its static inner *Builder* and *UnreadConversation* classes. The *Notification.CarExtender.Builder* has a constructor that requires a title for the extended notification. Its *addMessage()* method facilitates adding one or more messages to the *UnreadConversation*. The *setReadPendingIntent* method facilitates association with a *PendingIntent* that represents the read action. The *setReplyAction* method facilitates association with a *RemoteInput* object as well as a *PendingIntent* that represents the reply action. The unread conversation in turn encapsulates one or more messages as well as the names of the participants of the conversation.

Notification.CarExtender has an empty constructor and its *setUnreadConversation* method facilitates setting its *UnreadConversation* attribute. The *Notification.CarExtender* thus encapsulates an unread conversation and its encapsulated remote input as well as the read and reply intents.

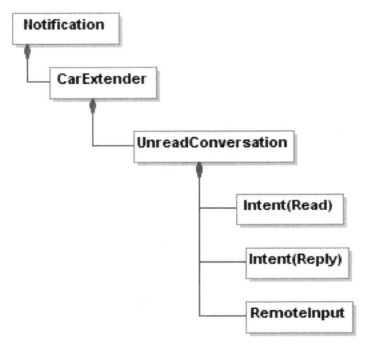

Figure **7-7** Notification, CarExtender, UnreadConversation, composition

Figure 7-7 attempts to denote diagrammatically, the composition relationship between a *Notification* extended to a *CarExtender*, which in turn is composed of the *UnreadConversation*.

Non-null read and reply Intents

Certain types of messages are inherently meant to be one-way messages, wherein the originating app or system has a need to provide some information, but does not need to solicit a response from the user. One such example may be a shipping system/app that needs to notify the user that a particular package has been delivered. In such one-way message scenarios, there is no relevance of remote input or a reply intent for response from the user. It is important to note that the current behavior of the *CarExtender* is such that it fails to deliver messages if the app originating the extended notification fails to call the *setReplyAction* on the *UnreadConversation* with a non-null reply intent and non-null remote input. It is thus important to be mindful of the fact that even if your app does not care for the remote input and reply action portion of the flow, it will need to provide a non null reply action. Otherwise the extension of the notification into *Android Auto* will fail in its entirety. For example, the Hello Auto(A) app from chapter 4 does not process the "reply" response, yet it was necessary to call the *setReplyAction* with a non-null action Intent in order to get the delivery of the read portion of the notification to work.

End To end Messaging Example

This section expands on the Hello Auto (A) app from chapter 4, to implement the capture of the remote input and make it available to the main application thats running in the phone. This is a nominal change, that closes the loop with respect to an end to end messaging implementation. The entry in the Android manifest for the broadcast receiver, that is associated with the "read" action is shown in the snippet below:

```
<receiver
  android:name=".MessageReadBroadcastReceiver">
  <intent-filter>
   <action
     android:name="info.androidautobook.messaginge2e.ACTION_READ" />
  </intent-filter>
</receiver>
```

The similar entry in the Android manifest for the broadcast receiver, that is associated with the "reply" action is shown in the snippet below:

```
<receiver
  android:name=".MessageReplyBroadcastReceiver">
  <intent-filter>
   <action
     android:name="info.androidautobook.messaginge2e.REPLY_ACTION"/>
  </intent-filter>
</receiver>
```

The broadcast receiver associated with "read" gets engaged when the message is read to the user, while the broadcast receiver associated with "reply" (*MessageReplyBroadcastReceiver*) gets engaged when the user replies to the message. In a real world messaging and communications application, the content of the voice input once received in the phone device may be sent to some cloud based endpoint. As this is a simple example, the content of the voice reply from the car extended notification is merely used to originate a notification for display on the phone only. This notification which represents the voice reply is not extended via car extender, therefore it will be seen by the user only after the user's device exits auto mode. The following snippet shows the implementation of the broadcast receiver associated with the remote input and the "reply" action:

```java
/**
 * This broadcast receiver class is associated with the reply action
 */
public class MessageReplyBroadcastReceiver extends BroadcastReceiver {
@Override
public void onReceive(Context context, Intent intent) {
    Log.d (TAG, "onReceive()..." + new Date()) ;
    String voiceReplyContent = "No reply";
    Bundle remoteInputBundle = RemoteInput.getResultsFromIntent(intent);
    Log.d (TAG, "onReceive() remoteInputBundle=" + remoteInputBundle) ;
    if (remoteInputBundle != null) {
            CharSequence charSequence =
                    remoteInputBundle.getCharSequence(EXTRA_VOICE_REPLY) ;
    voiceReplyContent = charSequence.toString() ;
}
Log.d (TAG, "onReceive()... voiceReplyContent=" + voiceReplyContent) ;
 // originate notification that will end up showing on the handheld
  Notification notification = new Notification.Builder(context)
        .setSmallIcon(R.drawable.alarm36)
        .setContentTitle("From Head unit")
        .setContentText (voiceReplyContent)
        .setColor (context.getResources().getColor(R.color.colorPrimary)).build() ;
    NotificationManager notificationManager =
            (NotificationManager)
                context.getSystemService(Context.NOTIFICATION_SERVICE);
  notificationManager.notify (referenceId, notification);
}
private static final String EXTRA_VOICE_REPLY = "EXTRA_VOICE_REPLY" ;
private static final String TAG = MessageReplyBroadcastReceiver.class.getName() ;
}
```

Figure 7-8 shows the notification – after exiting car-mode – in the hand-held device, that contains the content of the voice based remote input via the head-unit. Although this example did not use a service to deal with the messaging, most real world messaging apps that are enabled for *Android Auto* or otherwise typically do so. The next section covers an Android messaging service component.

Figure **7-8** Notification on hand-held device - content of remote input, voice reply

Notifications compatibility support

The *CarExtender* was introduced recently in the core Android framework API– in Android 6/API level 23. As the *CarExtender* is not available in the core Android 5 (API level 21) – platform that supports *Android Auto* – apps that support Android 5 (API level 21) devices benefit from *android.support.v4.app.NotificationCompat* – which is available in the v4 support library. *NotificationCompat* has much significance if you are supporting production apps that target a range of API levels including older ones that do not support particular extended notifications. As this book is future looking, it focuses on the exploration of the latest core Android API features, rather than support libraries for backward compatibility.

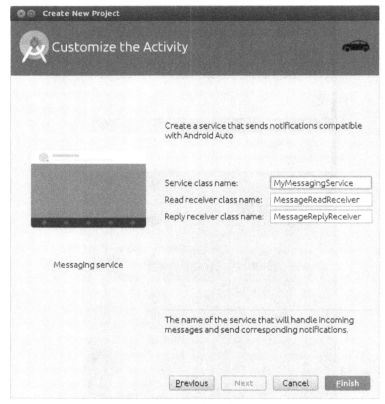

Figure 7-9 – Creating an Android Auto messaging app

The support libraries are fairly similar (though certainly not identical) to the core platform APIs. The details of *NotificationCompat* and *RemoteInput* from the support package are available at:

http://developer.android.com/reference/android/support/v4/app/NotificationCompat.html
http://developer.android.com/reference/android/support/v4/app/RemoteInput.html

As it turns out, Android Studio generates helpful cookie-cutter code for the *ReadIntent*, the *RepyIntent* and the *MessagingService* when you create an app thats enabled for Auto(messaging). This generated code is aligned with the v4 support library's

NotificationCompat and *RemoteInput*. The following snippet shows the generated code for the messaging service.

```java
public class MyMessagingService extends Service {

public static final String READ_ACTION =
            "info.androidautobook.myapplication.ACTION_MESSAGE_READ";
public  static final String REPLY_ACTION =
            "info.androidautobook.myapplication.ACTION_MESSAGE_REPLY";
public static final String CONVERSATION_ID = "conversation_id";
public static final String EXTRA_VOICE_REPLY = "extra_voice_reply";
private NotificationManagerCompat mNotificationManager;
private final Messenger mMessenger = new Messenger(new IncomingHandler());
/**
* Handler of incoming messages from clients.
*/
class IncomingHandler extends Handler {
@Override
public void handleMessage(Message msg) {
    sendNotification(1, "This is a sample message", "John Doe",
    System.currentTimeMillis());
}
}
@Override
public void onCreate() {
    mNotificationManager = NotificationManagerCompat.from(getApplicationContext());
}
@Override
public IBinder onBind(Intent intent) {
   return mMessenger.getBinder();
}
@Override
public int onStartCommand(Intent intent, int flags, int startId) {
   return START_STICKY;
}
private Intent createIntent(int conversationId, String action) {
            return new Intent()
              .addFlags(Intent.FLAG_INCLUDE_STOPPED_PACKAGES)
              .setAction(action)
              .putExtra(CONVERSATION_ID, conversationId);
}
private void sendNotification(int conversationId, String message,
   String participant, long timestamp) {
// A pending Intent for reads
PendingIntent readPendingIntent = PendingIntent.getBroadcast(getApplicationContext(),
conversationId,
```

```
            createIntent(conversationId, READ_ACTION),
            PendingIntent.FLAG_UPDATE_CURRENT);
    // Build a RemoteInput for receiving voice input in a Car Notification
    RemoteInput remoteInput = new RemoteInput.Builder(EXTRA_VOICE_REPLY)
      .setLabel("Reply by voice")
      .build();
    // Building a Pending Intent for the reply action to trigger
    PendingIntent replyIntent = PendingIntent.getBroadcast(getApplicationContext(),
            conversationId,
            createIntent(conversationId, REPLY_ACTION),
            PendingIntent.FLAG_UPDATE_CURRENT);
    // Create UnreadConversation , populate it with the participant name,
    // read and reply intents.
     UnreadConversation.Builder unreadConvBuilder =
         new UnreadConversation.Builder(participant)
         .setLatestTimestamp(timestamp)
         .setReadPendingIntent(readPendingIntent)
         .setReplyAction(replyIntent, remoteInput);

    NotificationCompat.Builder builder = new NotificationCompat.Builder(getApplicationContext())
        .setContentText(message)
        .setWhen(timestamp)
        .setContentTitle(participant)
        .setContentIntent(readPendingIntent)
        .extend(new CarExtender()
        .setUnreadConversation(unreadConvBuilder.build()));
     mNotificationManager.notify(conversationId, builder.build());
     }
    private static final String TAG = MyMessagingService.class.getSimpleName();
     }
```

Android Auto App, Play Services App – under the covers

When the driver's Android phone gets connected to an *Android Auto* compatible head-unit unit via USB, the *Google Play Services app* and the *Android Auto protocol library* that is running in the head-unit, establish a handshake over the *Android Auto protocol* . (You may refer again to Figure 2-4 *Android Auto protocol, head-unit, apps* in Chapter 2 on page 22.) As long as the phone and the head-unit are engaged in *Android Auto mode*, the *Android Auto protocol library* remains active in the head-unit. The *Android Auto App* and the *Play Services app* ensure that the phone goes into car-mode during which time the *Android Auto* logo is displayed while the phone screen is disabled for touch input. The head-unit screen in turn gets activated and its display and audio systems respectively provide projected visual and sound output information to the driver per the data received by the *Android Auto protocol library* over the USB connection. The *protocol library* ensures that the user inputs via touch and voice into the automobile head-unit's touch screen and micro-phone, the steering wheel inputs (such as volume control), and live car sensor data sent over the *Android Auto protocol* to the phone via the USB connection. As long as the phone remains in car-mode, the *Play Services app* monitors car extended notifications and media playback events, across all installed apps that are *Android Auto* enabled and makes them available to the head-unit via the *Android Auto protocol library* as needed. The *Android Auto protocol* based connection is bi-directional and multiplexed.

In conclusion, this chapter covered the APIs pertinent to extending messages and notifications to Android Auto.

References and further reading

http://developer.android.com/training/auto/messaging/index.html
http://developer.android.com/preview/features/notification-updates.html
https://support.google.com/nexus/answer/6111295?hl=en
https://developer.android.com/reference/android/app/Notification.CarExtender.html
https://developer.android.com/reference/android/app/Notification.CarExtender.UnreadConversation.html
http://developer.android.com/reference/android/content/Intent.html
http://developer.android.com/reference/android/app/PendingIntent.html
http://developer.android.com/reference/android/app/Notification.html#FLAG_ONGOING_EVENT
http://developer.android.com/reference/android/app/Notification.html
https://www.google.com/design/spec-auto/audio-apps/audio-app-anatomy.html
https://www.google.com/design/spec-auto/messaging-apps/voice-based-messaging.html
http://developer.android.com/training/wearables/notifications/voice-input.html

CHAPTER 8

Media/Audio Apps

This chapter covers Android's media APIs that are pertinent to audio playback, as well as the steps involved in extending an Android application's media playback functions into *Android Auto*. If any of your existing Android apps pertain to audio books, recorded talks, or music, you may consider extending them to *Android Auto* as media(audio) apps. You may also think of a new audio app that is suitable for driving and does not introduce distraction.

Android media API

Media is a broad term that includes photo, video, audio and camera related functions – all of which have deep support in the base Android APIs. *Android Auto* allows media apps to extend their audio related functionality, but particularly excludes video display functions – in the interest of minimizing driver distraction.

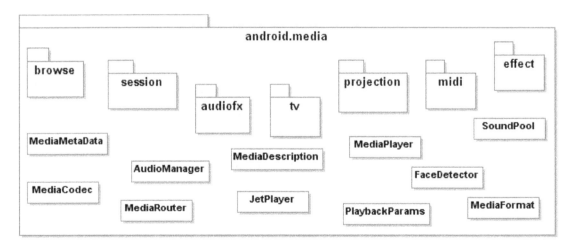

Figure **8-1** *media* package, sub-packages and classes (partial listing)

android.media package

The *android.media* package contains classes, interfaces, and sub-packages that are pertinent to audio, video and camera, playback and recording. Figure 8-1 lists the sub-packages and a few of the classes that reside directly under the *android.media* namespace, such as *MediaMetaData*, *MediaDescription*, *MediaPlayer*, and *AudioManager*. The *MediaMetaData* class provides metadata about the media such as the name of the artist, title of the album, the number of tracks in an album, and year of release. The *MediaPlayer* class provides control of playback of audio and video files and streams. *AudioManager* is an Android system service that provides access to volume control.

MediaBrowserService, android.service.media package

MediaBrowserService is an abstract class that serves as the base class for implementing media browser services which enable applications to browse media content. Your media browser service implementation must be declared in the Android manifest with the intent filter action *MediaBrowserService.SERVICE_INTERFACE* which has a string value of *android.media.browse.MediaBrowserService*.

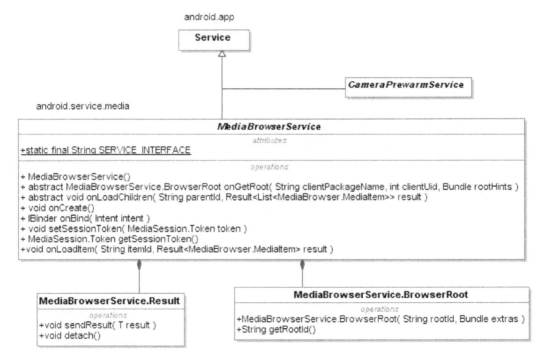

Figure **8-2** MediaBrowserService class in android.service.media package, partial listing

Figure 8-2 shows the *MediaBrowserService* class and its inner classes *BrowserRoot* and *Result*. *BrowserRoot* encapsulates information that the *MediaBrowserService* implementation needs to send when a client first connects to it.

142

MediaBrowser

MediaBrowser is a class that allows applications to connect to a *MediaBrowserService* component. Figure 8-3 shows the *MediaBrowser* and its inner classes *ConnectionCallBack*, *MediaItem*, *ItemCallback*, and *SubscriptionCallback*.

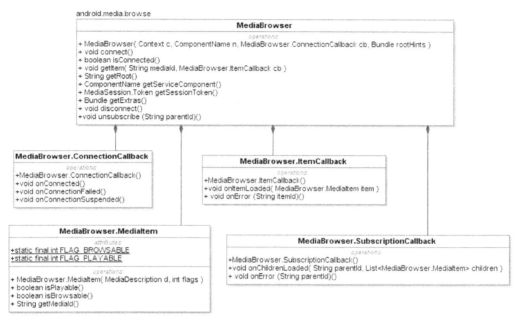

Figure **8-3** *browse* sub-package, MediaBrowser class

MediaBrowser can be directly instantiated, but is not thread-safe -- it is meant to be used only by the thread that instantiated it. Once an application establishes a connection to its associated *MediaBrowserService*, a *MediaSession* is established which allows the application to control the media via the *MediaController.* The application can also subscribe to changes in media content as well as error conditions via the *SubscriptionCallback* methods. *MediaItem* may be playable or browsable; browsable indicates that the *MediaItem* may have children in the content tree. *ItemCallback* allows the application to discern when the media item has been returned from the *MediaBrowserService,* or if any error has occurred.

MediaController

The class *MediaController* is a view that provides the user with the ability to control media playback; it also typically displays the current status and progress of the playback. Applications can instantiate *MediaController* which creates a default set of controls and places them in a window that floats above the application view that is set via the *setAnchorView()* method. Figure 8-4 shows the *MediaController* and its inner *MediaPlayerControl* class.

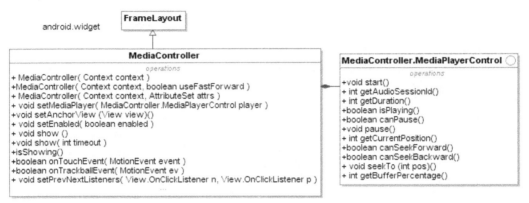

Figure **8-4** MediaController class

MediaPlayer

The *MediaPlayer* class lies at the heart of media playback of audio (as well as video) files and streams. Playback control is implemented as a state machine, with discrete states and state transitions such as *Idle, Initialized, Prepared, Started, Stopped, Paused, Completed Playback*. Elaborate and elegant explanations on the media player are available at the Android developer site:

http://developer.android.com/guide/topics/media/mediaplayer.html, and
http://developer.android.com/reference/android/media/MediaPlayer.html

Figure 8-5 reproduces – for ready reference – a really useful diagram from the first of the references above, that shows the media player's states and state transitions. Also, a useful guide on extending an app as an Android Auto media app is available at:

http://developer.android.com/training/auto/audio/index.html

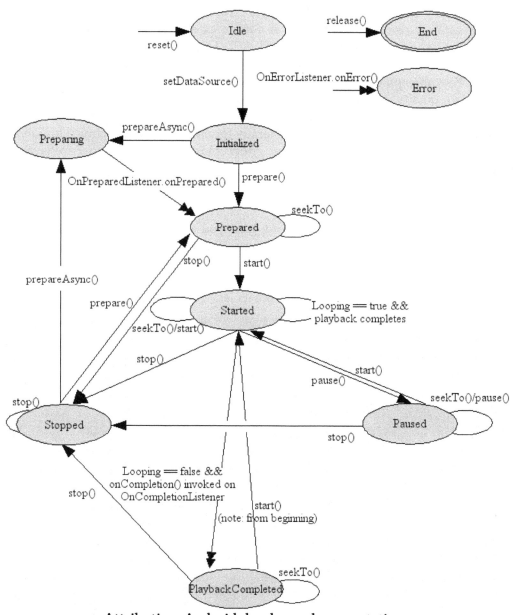

Attribution: Android developer documentation
http://developer.android.com/images/mediaplayer_state_diagram.gif
Figure **8-5** MediaPlayer, state diagram

ExoPlayer

ExoPlayer is an open source media player from Google. It resides in the package *com.google.android.exoplayer* and serves as a more extensible and customizable alternative to the *MediaPlayer* from the core Android API. ExoPlayer supports Dynamic Adaptive Streaming over HTTP (DASH) and adaptive playback and is used in Google's own apps such as the Youtube app on Android. DASH is an adaptive bitrate streaming technique that supports high quality streaming of media content delivered over conventional HTTP servers. As ExoPlayer is external to the core Android API, it can be updated along with app updates via the Play Store. ExoPlayer is generally found to be a better choice for any serious Android media playback app development effort. More information on ExpPlayer can be found at: https://github.com/google/ExoPlayer.

Extending audio apps to Android Auto

In order to extend an audio app to *Android Auto*, you will need to ensure that it includes a *MediaBrowserService* implementation. Your app will need to provide media browse and playback interface implementations and declare via manifest entries, its interest in getting extended to *Android Auto* as an audio service provider. Doing so will allow the *Android Auto* platform to discover your app and make its launcher available via the user's head-unit.

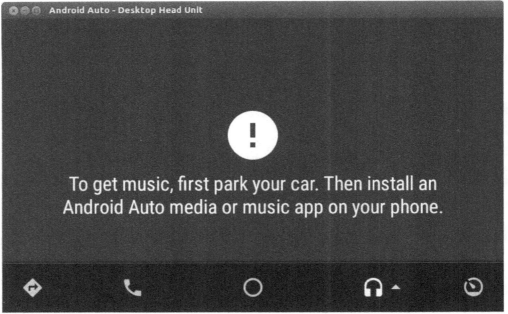

Figure **8-6A** Accessing Audio service providers - no provider

Depending on the user's in-vehicle inputs, the Android Auto platform will ensure that the playback related requests reach your app. Even before we dive into the development steps, let us explore the user experience and perspective with regard to the availability of and access to audio apps via the head-unit.

In order to list the apps on your Android phone that serve as Audio service providers for the *Android Auto* platform, you will need to access the Audio section in the Android Auto head-unit represented by the head-set icon. In case your Android device does not have any audio app that is implemented as an Audio service provider extended to *Android Auto*, you will not be able to access audio functions in your car (Figure 8-6A).

Thus, audio functions become available to you on your *Android Auto* head-unit only if you have the Google Play Music (which is but naturally extended to *Android Auto*) or any other audio app that has been extended to *Android Auto,* installed and available on your phone. If your Android device has one or more audio apps that have been implemented as an audio service provider extended to *Android Auto*, you will see it listed as a music app in *Android Auto*, as shown in Figure 8-6B.

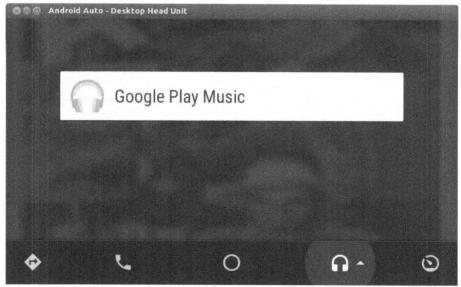

Figure **8-6B** Accessing Audio service providers - one provider Google Play Music

In order to extend your audio app to Android Auto, you will need to declare your app as an automotive media app in the Android manifest and ensure that your audio player is implemented as a *MediaBrowserService*, as elaborated in the sample app that follows.

MuziKar sample app

The *Muzikar app* which is part of this book's sample code, is an Android Auto enabled audio app. The following entry in it's Android manifest tells the Android platform of its intention to be extended to *Android Auto* as a media app:

```xml
<meta-data
  android:name="com.google.android.gms.car.application"
  android:resource="@xml/automotive_app_desc" />
```

The content of the *automotive_app_desc.xml* resource referenced in the Android manifest's *meta-data* entry is as under:

```xml
<?xml version="1.0" encoding="utf-8"?>
<automotiveApp>
 <uses name="media"/>
</automotiveApp>
```

The *MuzikarMusicService* implements the *MediaBrowserService* which will require an entry in the Android manifest as is the case for any application Service component:

```xml
<service
  android:name=".MuziKarMusicService"
  android:exported="true" >
 <intent-filter>
 <action
 android:name="android.media.browse.MediaBrowserService" />
 </intent-filter>
</service>
```

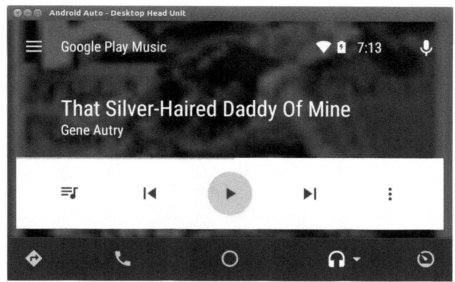

Figure 8-7A Accessing Audio service providers

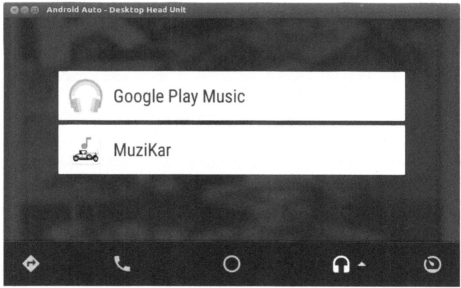

Figure **8-7B** Audio service provider – MuziKar example app

As soon as you have the above basic manifest entries and skeleton service component in place, installing your app on your phone and will allow you to see your app easily engage with the Android Auto platform/ DHU as a music service app(Figures 8-7A and 8-7B).

It is essential for your *MediaBrowserService* service implementation to have its *exported* flag set to *true* – as this will allow other applications to invoke and interact with your service.

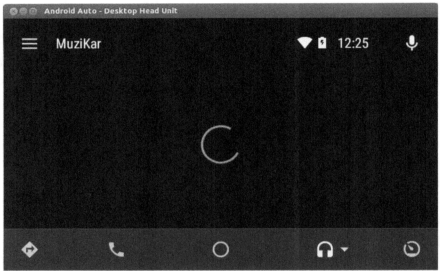

Figure **8-8A** MuziKar skeleton app

Figure 8-8A and 8-8B show the Muzikar skeleton app's user interfaces displayed in the head-unit. It does not play anything yet – as the code implements trivial methods merely to be compliant with the required interface contracts in *MediaBrowserService*.

I used the approach of progressively filling in richer method implementations as a means to study the cause and effect relationships between the methods and corresponding imparted application behaviors.

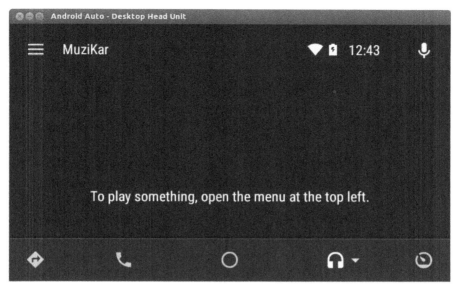

Figure **8-8B** MuziKar skeleton app

For now, the following is the skeleton implementation of the *MuzikarMusicService* that corresponds to the user interfaces shown in Figures 8-8A and 8-8 B.

```
public class MuziKarMusicService extends MediaBrowserService
      implements OnPreparedListener, OnCompletionListener,
        OnErrorListener, AudioManager.OnAudioFocusChangeListener {
 private MediaSession mediaSession;
 private MediaPlayer mediaPlayer;
 private List<MediaSession.QueueItem> playingQueue;
 @Override
 public void onCreate() {
  super.onCreate();
  Log.d ( TAG, "onCreate() ..." ) ;
  mediaSession = new MediaSession(this, "MuziKarMusicService");
  setSessionToken(mediaSession.getSessionToken());
  mediaSession.setCallback(new MediaSessionCallback());
  mediaSession.setFlags(MediaSession.FLAG_HANDLES_MEDIA_BUTTONS |
  MediaSession.FLAG_HANDLES_TRANSPORT_CONTROLS);
 }
 @Override
 public void onDestroy() {
  Log.d ( TAG, "onDestroy() ..." ) ;
  mediaSession.release();
```

```java
}
@Override
public BrowserRoot onGetRoot(String clientPackageName, int clientUid,
                            Bundle rootHints) {
 Log.d ( TAG, "onGetRoot() ... returning " +
 this.musicSource.getRoot() ) ;
 return new BrowserRoot(this.musicSource.getRoot(), null);
}
@Override
public void onLoadChildren(final String parentMediaId,
 final Result<List<MediaItem>> result) {
 Log.d(TAG, "onLoadChildren() ... returning" +
 this.musicSource.getMediaItems() ) ;
 result.sendResult(this.musicSource.getMediaItems());
}

private final class MediaSessionCallback extends MediaSession.Callback{
@Override
public void onPlay() {
 Log.d ( TAG, "onPlay() ..." ) ;
}
@Override
public void onSkipToQueueItem(long queueId) {
 Log.d ( TAG, "onSkipToQueueItem() ..." ) ;
}
@Override
public void onSeekTo(long position) {
 Log.d ( TAG, "onSeekTo() ..." ) ;
}
@Override
public void onPlayFromMediaId(String mediaId, Bundle extras) {
 Log.d ( TAG, "ononPlayFromMediaId() ..." ) ;
}
@Override
public void onPause() {
}
@Override
public void onStop() {
}
@Override
public void onSkipToNext() {
}
@Override
public void onSkipToPrevious() {
}
@Override
public void onCustomAction(String action, Bundle extras) {
```

```
}
@Override
public void onPlayFromSearch(final String query,
                      final Bundle extras) {

}
}
@Override
public void onPrepared(MediaPlayer player) {

}
@Override
public void onCompletion(MediaPlayer player) {

}
@Override
public boolean onError(MediaPlayer mp, int what, int extra) {
 boolean retVal = false ;
 return retVal ;
}
/**
 * audiomanager --> focuschanges
 */
@Override
public void onAudioFocusChange(int focusChange) {
}
 private static final String TAG = MuziKarMusicService.class.toString() ;
}
```

I created a class to encapsulate the music content thats available as a raw resource file located in the application's *res/raw* directory.

```
public class MusicSource {
 private final String [] GENRE = {"FOLK", "CLASSICAL"} ;
 private final String SONG_PREFIX = "android.resource://" +
                  BuildConfig.APPLICATION_ID + "/" ;
 private TreeMap <String, MediaMetadata> musicCollection =
            new TreeMap< String, MediaMetadata>() ;
  private int currentSong = 1 ;
 public MusicSource() {
  init();
 }
 public void init () {
  Log.d(TAG, "init() entered") ;
  MediaMetadata aMediaMetadata = new MediaMetadata.Builder()
  .putString(MediaMetadata.METADATA_KEY_MEDIA_ID, "1")
  .putString(MediaMetadata.METADATA_KEY_GENRE, GENRE[0])
  .putString(MediaMetadata.METADATA_KEY_TITLE,
```

```java
                  "Prelude in C Major")
         .putString(MediaMetadata.METADATA_KEY_ARTIST,
                   "Johann Sebastian Bach")
        .build();
   musicCollection.put ("1", aMediaMetadata) ;
   aMediaMetadata = new MediaMetadata.Builder()
        .putString(MediaMetadata.METADATA_KEY_MEDIA_ID, "2")
        .putString(MediaMetadata.METADATA_KEY_GENRE, GENRE[1])
        .putString(MediaMetadata.METADATA_KEY_TITLE,
                     "The Blue Danube")
        .putString(MediaMetadata.METADATA_KEY_COMPOSER, "Johann Strauss II")
        .build();
musicCollection.put ("2", aMediaMetadata);
aMediaMetadata = new MediaMetadata.Builder()
   .putString(MediaMetadata.METADATA_KEY_MEDIA_ID, "3")
   .putString(MediaMetadata.METADATA_KEY_GENRE, GENRE[1])
   .putString(MediaMetadata.METADATA_KEY_TITLE,
                     "Thoughts are free")
   .putString(MediaMetadata.METADATA_KEY_COMPOSER,
        "Andreas, Franz, Gunter & Thomas")
   .build();
musicCollection.put ("3", aMediaMetadata);
Log.d( TAG, "init() done this.musicCollection size=" +
                     this.musicCollection.size() ) ;
}
public String getRoot() {
return "" ;
}
public List<MediaBrowser.MediaItem> getMediaItems() {
 List<MediaBrowser.MediaItem> retVal =
       new ArrayList<MediaBrowser.MediaItem>();
 MediaBrowser.MediaItem newMediaItem = null ;
 for (MediaMetadata aMetadata: this.musicCollection.values()) {
  newMediaItem =
       new MediaBrowser.MediaItem( aMetadata.getDescription(),
                 MediaBrowser.MediaItem.FLAG_PLAYABLE) ;
  retVal.add( newMediaItem) ;
 }
return retVal ;
}
public String getSongUri(String mediaId) {
 return SONG_PREFIX + mediaId ;
}
public String getSongUri() {
 String mediaId = Integer.toString( currentSong) ;
 currentSong = currentSong++ ;
```

```
   return SONG_PREFIX + mediaId ;
 }
 public String getNextSongUri() {
  int nextSong = currentSong +1 ;
  if ( nextSong > this.musicCollection.size() ) {
  nextSong = 1 ;
 }
 if ( nextSong <=0 ) {
  nextSong = 1 ;
 }
 String mediaId = Integer.toString( nextSong) ;
  currentSong = nextSong ;
 return SONG_PREFIX + mediaId ;
 }
 private static final String TAG = MusicSource.class.getName() ;
```

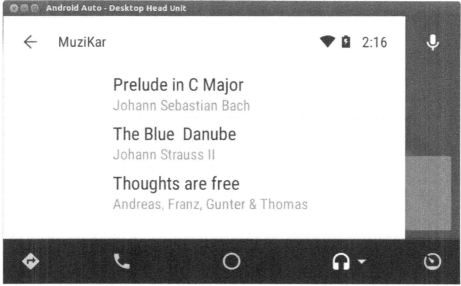

Figure **8-8C** MuziKar app, media items listed via left navigation drawer

At this point, the *MuzikarMusicService* source code as shown in the previous pages includes a non-trivial implementation for the `onLoadChildren()` method which provides a collection of songs. Figure 8-8C shows the listing of songs upon accessing the navigation menu on the top left. As the *MuzikarMusicService* does not yet include non-trivial functional implementations for the media playback supporting methods, tapping on a song does not result in playback (it does not result in any errors or application instability either).

The next step in this incremental development effort entails implementing the various callbacks from *MediaBrowserServices* and *MediaSession* and supporting code. The most significant of these is the *onPlayFromMediaId* method in *MuziKarMusicService*.

```java
@Override
public void onPlayFromMediaId(String mediaId, Bundle extras) {
 Log.d(TAG, "MediaSessionCallback onPlayFromMediaId() ... mediaId =" +
                              mediaId) ;
 if ( mediaPlayer == null ) {
 mediaPlayer = new MediaPlayer();
 Log.d ( TAG, "MediaSessionCallback onPlayFromMediaId() created
                                  mediaPlayer =" + mediaPlayer ) ;
 }
 try {
 mediaPlayer.setAudioStreamType(AudioManager.STREAM_MUSIC);
  mediaPlayer.setOnCompletionListener
               (myMediaPlayerOnCompletionListener);
  mediaPlayer.setWakeMode( getApplicationContext(),
                   PowerManager.PARTIAL_WAKE_LOCK);
  mediaPlayer.setDataSource(getApplicationContext(),
                      Uri.parse(musicSource.getSongUri(mediaId))) ;
  Log.d(TAG, "MediaSessionCallback onPlayFromMediaId() …
    mediaPlayer setDataSource " + musicSource.getSongUri(mediaId)) ;
  Log.d(TAG, "MediaSessionCallback onPlayFromMediaId() …
                              about to prepareAsync() ") ;
  mediaPlayer.prepareAsync();
  Log.d(TAG, "MediaSessionCallback onPlayFromMediaId()
                                 ...about to start ") ;
  mediaSession.setActive(true);
  mediaSession.setMetadata( musicSource.getMediaMetaData( mediaId));
  mediaPlayer.start();
 } catch ( Exception e) {
  Log.e ( TAG, "MediaSessionCallback onPlayFromMediaId()
  exception e=" + e) ;
 }
}
```

Figure 8-8D shows the *MuziKar app* playing a song with basic playback controls for pause, previous and next.

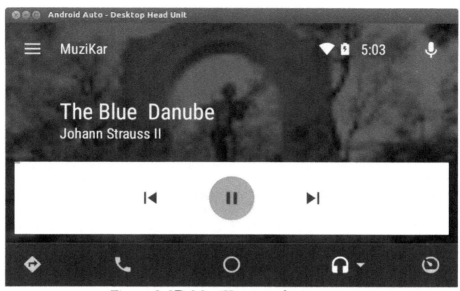
Figure **8-8D** MuziKar app playing song

An Android Auto media app can become aware when it the user connects(uses) and disconnects from it as a media app in the head-unit – via the broadcast intent action *com.google.android.gms.car.media.STATUS*. The complete source code for this application which is available in this book's source code repository includes the detection of the media connect/disconnect status.

Also, Google has an elaborate sample app, the universal Music player which serves as an excellent reference on media playback across various devices such as hand-held, *Android Wear, Google Cast* devices, and *Android Auto*, the source code for which can be found at https://github.com/googlesamples/android-UniversalMusicPlayer.

In conclusion, this chapter covered the APIs pertinent and a sample app pertinent to media playback functions on Android Auto.

References and further reading

http://developer.android.com/training/auto/audio/index.html
http://developer.android.com/guide/topics/media/mediaplayer.html
http://developer.android.com/reference/android/media/MediaPlayer.html
http://developer.android.com/reference/android/media/browse/MediaBrowser.html
https://en.wikipedia.org/wiki/Dynamic_Adaptive_Streaming_over_HTTP
https://en.wikipedia.org/wiki/Adaptive_bitrate_streaming
https://github.com/google/ExoPlayer
https://www.youtube.com/watch?v=6VjF638VObA
http://developer.android.com/training/auto/audio/index.html
https://github.com/googlesamples/android-UniversalMusicPlayer
https://www.google.com/cast/

Part V   THE ROAD AHEAD

This provides insight into ecosystem of the automobile and transportation and connects the dots of the trends across human, technological, legal, and socio-economic factors. It covers the synergistic effects of technological advancements such as collision avoidance systems, self-driving cars, in conjunction with the social trends of rising car sharing and declining rates of automobile ownership.

CHAPTER 9   Future directions

The *Android Auto* platform is for the most part influenced by, dependent on, and fits into the wider ecosystem of the automobile, transportation, and infotainment – as a new entrant. While this chapter covers some of the likely features that *Android Auto* may support in the near future, it also ventures into the many current and emerging trends in the ecosystem of the automobile, automotive computing, infotainment, and personal transportation. It takes a broad view of the technological, social, economic, civic and legal trends that influence the evolution of the ecosystem of personal transportation.

In-vehicle & consumer digital computing ecosystems

While smart phones reached the hands of consumers relatively recently, on-board diagnostics computer systems were introduced into vehicles in the late 1960s and became more widely used in the early 1980s. Volkswagen, Datsun(Nissan) and General Motors were some of the early adopters of on-board diagnostic computer systems. Today, the computational ecosystem within a modern vehicle is diverse and complex. The execution of the modern automobile's core functions are dependent on a diversity of computing systems. The infotainment system can be considered to reside at the edge of the modern automobile's computational ecosystem. The infotainment system of most modern vehicles represents a minuscule percentage of the total computation power that resides inside the vehicle.

Both the consumer digital and computing ecosystem (that includes the Internet, cloud and mobile devices) and the automobile computing ecosystem (that includes the vehicular computing system) have been evolving independently for decades. Today, these two ecosystems are poised for meaningful integration. Some of the core computational system's built-in diagnostics may have relevance for integration with the head-unit and upstream to the phone and the user. The head-unit can serve as a gateway for making relevant vehicle data available to the consumer ecosystem, based on which timely suggestions can be made to the consumer, that boost driver convenience – without introducing irrelevant distractions or compromising safety. The head-unit also serves as a bridge that can get vehicular data into the smart phone and to the cloud for meaningful analysis and utilization – subject to the user's authorization and participation.

Personal computing devices and platforms tend to evolve rather rapidly and have a low barrier to reaching the hands of consumers quickly, for example many smart phone users are able to switch to newer models every year. Automobiles too tend to evolve somewhat rapidly but their size, cost and complexity makes them slightly slower evolving than personal computing devices. The pace of innovation and change in the automobile has accelerated, as more of the automobile has gotten dependent on computing technology and the many advanced features that it can bring. The paradigm of the long term multi-year association between an individual consumer and a particular instance of an automobile in a ownership or leasing model tends to make it more difficult for automobile enthusiasts to experience the latest automobile technological advancements in a convenient and economical manner.

In recent years, the automobile's core operational functions have come to depend on more advanced embedded computing devices and algorithms. As more embedded system computing power becomes available at lower prices, more advanced algorithms and sophisticated safety and convenience features become possible. In the years to come, the power and capabilities of the automobile's computing system are expected to increase even more significantly. In the meantime, many trends have been emerging in recent years such as ride sharing, online vehicle rentals, and last but not least, self-driving cars. There is a general trend away from car ownership and towards alternatives such as car sharing, urban living, walking, biking, and public transport especially among the millennial generation in the United States. "Peak car" is a hypothesis that the number of vehicles in active use has peaked and will decline in the coming years and decades.

Since the invention of the motor car and the success of its mass manufacturing and mass consumer adoption, since a hundred years ago, the fundamentals of the car has remained fundamentally unchanged. Although car models have certainly evolved year over year in a rather competitive market place, the paradigm of car purchase, ownership, leasing, financing and the typical multi-year individual car ownership life cycle have been relatively unchanged until very recently. Today, it is widely acknowledged that significant changes are underway, due to the convergence of many factors across many diverse domains. The stage is set for a new revolution in the ecosystem of the automobile and transportation and there is much excitement today about the future of consumer transportation.

Android Auto platform - incremental expansion

The *Android Auto* platform in its initial version – and the current version, at the time of writing – is limited to a minimal set of relevant essential functions and capabilities. Over time, it is inevitable that Google and the rest of the members of the *Open Automotive Alliance* will consider expanding the base functions of the *Android Auto* platform, as well as permit additional relevant application functions to be extended to it. There is potential for metrics collection and back-end data analytics based integration that is not head-unit user interface centric. It is also possible that *Android Auto* will integrate or interoperate with other open standards such as *SmartDeviceLink*. Whenever new feature expansions are considered, there is much analysis and evaluation that is expectedly carried out often unbeknownst to the consumer, in order to ensure that the fundamental criteria of boosting driver safety, improving driver convenience, and limiting distraction are met.

Base platform expansion

In general, the more the consumer ecosystem and the automobile are made to engage meaningfully, the greater the convenience to the driver/consumer. In the new world of the IoT, it is important for automobile manufacturer and hardware device makers to engage with the rest of the user's digital ecosystem in a device independent and non-proprietary manner. Consumers will tend to appreciate their automobile from a digital standpoint, if it is easy for the rest of their digital ecosystem to have access to relevant data. Openness generally ends up as a win-win for consumers, auto-makers and leading Internet platforms alike. There are several key nuggets of vehicle data, discussed below, that the driver needs to routinely keep track of, and take necessary or remedial action as needed. Such nuggets of vehicle data become more useful and valuable when they are readily available to the consumer's digital ecosystem that includes locations, maps, driving destinations, contacts, phone calls, messaging, and intelligent personal assistants.

Fuel level, mileage, speed

As I write this sentence, I have no idea how much gas is in my car's fuel tank at this moment. The only way I can find out is to head to my garage and enter my vehicle and turn on the ignition. Many drivers have experienced the undesirable coincidence of needing to fill gas at the most inopportune time with respect to our personal schedule that is typically quite hectic. At some point automobile manufacturers will prioritize making fuel tank data readily available to their consumer's favorite digital platforms. An *Android Auto* platform that has access to fuel tank data will gain the ability to make timely recommendation to fill gas – along with fuel/service station destinations. Also, the detour-distance to the service stations with respect to regular driving routes in conjunction, with the gas price, as well as consumer's personal preferences (cost versus time) can be useful factors in generating fuel/service station destination recommendations.

On an impulse, I attempted to peek at the available runtime permissions of all the apps on my Android device that pertain to CAR or AUTO. Running the following *pm list permissions* command on my development computer, while connected to my Nexus 6 Android phone :

```
adb shell pm list permissions -g | grep CAR | grep google
```

yielded some relevant and interesting information, shown in Figure 9-1 below:

```
~ $ adb shell pm list permissions -g | grep CAR | grep -v CARD | grep google
group:com.google.android.gms.permission.CAR_INFORMATION
  permission:com.google.android.gms.permission.CAR_VENDOR_EXTENSION
  permission:com.google.android.gms.permission.CAR_MILEAGE
  permission:com.google.android.gms.permission.CAR_FUEL
  permission:com.google.android.gms.permission.CAR_SPEED
  permission:com.google.android.gms.permission.CAR
~ $ █
```

Figure **9-1** CAR permissions in Google Play Service app, on my Nexus 6 device

A closer inspection of permissions indicated to me that there are two relevant permission groups and associated group member permissions as shown below:

```
group:com.google.android.gms.permission.CAR_INFORMATION
  permission:com.google.android.gms.permission.CAR_VENDOR_EXTENSION
  permission:com.google.android.gms.permission.CAR_MILEAGE
  permission:com.google.android.gms.permission.CAR_FUEL
```

```
group:android.permission-group.LOCATION
  permission:android.permission.ACCESS_FINE_LOCATION
  permission:com.google.android.gms.permission.CAR_SPEED
  permission:android.permission.ACCESS_COARSE_LOCATION
```

There is also a stand-alone permission :

```
permission:com.google.android.gms.permission.CAR
```

This indicates that we are likely to see car mileage, car fuel, and also vendor specific extensions in the near future. I could not find any corresponding documentation on Google's Android developer or *Android Auto* developer resources regarding car mileage, fuel levels or vendor enhancements. The namespace *com.google.android.gms* corresponds to the Google Play services app that is available in the Play store at: https://play.google.com/store/apps/details?id=com.google.android.gms which supports many diverse functions including updating other installed apps from the Play store (including apps by Google such as the *Android Auto App*), authenticating to Google back end services, application functions pertaining to maps and location, phone, messaging, payments, *Android Wear*, *Google Fit*, and *Android Auto*. The namespace *com.google.android.gms.car* pertains to the core *Android Auto* related functions and resides within the implementation of Google Play services that resides and executes on the consumer's phone. An examination of my Android phone's adb log file showed many classes in the package *com.google.android.gms.car* such as *Car, CarActivity, CarCall, CarInfo, CarLog, CarAudioRecord, CarAudioTrack, CarCall, CarUiInfo, CarPhoneStatus, CarSensorEvent, CarAudioConfiguration, CarAudioManager, CarNotSupportedException, CarVendorExtensionManager* as well as many corresponding Android AIDL artifacts such as *ICar, ICarSensor* to name just a few. Google's publicly available API documentation for the package *com.google.android.gms* available at: https://developers.google.com/android/reference/com/google/android/gms/package-summary currently excludes the *car* sub-package, which thus has no available documentation. Other than a few *meta-data* elements that *Android Auto* applications may use in their manifest such as: *com.google.android.gms.car.application, com.google.android.gms.car.media.STATUS,* and *com.google.android.gms.car.SmallIcon*, the classes and interfaces in the *gms.car* sub-package are not meant to be used directly by your application – though it is certainly possible that in the future, Google will open some of these for application use, with the user's consent.

The availability of vehicle information to third party apps has great potential to enable back end integration, analytics, and recommendations pertaining to the automobile and driving, free from the constraints seen in head-unit user interface oriented applications. There is also potential for the sharing of vehicle information with other consumers as well as other businesses with the user's consent, such as the sharing of diagnostic information with the consumer's preferred automobile maintenance and servicing provider, and/or speed and mileage information with an auto insurance provider. In a world of IoT, with a large multitude of connected computing devices and equipment per user/consumer, it wouldn't make sense if each connected device required its own separate app and/or "alien" digital platform; most consumers already have one or more "favorite" widely used digital/Internet platform(s). Irrespective of any digital platform that any given automobile maker may build themselves, it would be equally relevant that consumer automobile data be made available via open APIs so that popular user centric platforms may access these if the user/consumer so prefers.

Maintenance warning integration

Automobiles typically come equipped with maintenance warning lights in the main instrument cluster that is located right in front of the driver's field of vision. The remedial action in response to a warning light might entail a trip to the service station or a phone call. Drivers will surely appreciate a smooth, integrated integration that presents relevant suggest cards for placing a phone call and/or driving directions to a nearby service station.

Application function extension

Currently – at the time of writing – the *Android Auto* platform does not permit the extension of third party application's phone dialer or navigation functions. It it possible that at some later point, there will be support for these functions.

Most applications that provide map functions including driving directions leverage the Google Maps API that is used by Google Map app. For the most part, extension of application map functionality into *Android Auto* will likely duplicate functions provided by Google Maps, and the overlay of other domain specific functions such as home buying or deals and coupons for example, will tend to be distracting while driving. However, the category of the professional driver navigation is an obvious case that has merits for extension to *Android Auto*.

Professional Driver navigation

There are currently many driver navigation apps that professional drivers in the service or delivery industry use in order to carry out their daily driving work. Often times, such apps run on generic devices that are mounted independently, without leveraging the vehicle's head-unit. Permitting the extension of map functions of professional driver apps to *Android Auto*, will enable professional drivers to benefit from *Android Auto*'s integration with the head-unit, steering wheel based controls and the consistent design and safety standards that the *Android Auto* platform enforces – which are themselves based on various national and local driving safety standards.

Automobiles - core computational ecosystem

Over the last few decades, automobile manufacturers have been gradually introducing drive-by-wire technology which performs many critical functions such as control of brakes, transmissions, airbags, throttle, and more. Although many of the automobile's human-machine interfaces in modern vehicles continue to remain mechanical in nature, the driver's mechanical inputs – in a drive-by-wire system – get converted into corresponding electrical signals. As an example, the position of the accelerator pedal may be measured by a sensor whose signal is interpreted by a computing control unit which in turn sends electronic signals to a computer controlled actuator that controls fuel injection. The carburetor – a device that controls fuel injection into the combustion engine, and was invented in the 1800s – began to be replaced in recent decades by electronic fuel injection technology which is more efficient.

The use of drive-by-wire has many advantages including lower cost and better fuel efficiency due to reduction of heavy mechanical linkages such as steering column, shafts and hoses. The reduction of mechanical linkages has enormous benefits in terms of precision, reliability, fuel economy, and performance. An automobile with an internal ecosystem that is dependent on computing devices for carrying out its core functions, is one that is conducive to the introduction of additional computational resources and algorithms that implement advanced driver assistance, safety and convenience features. In recent years, a variety of such driver safety and assistance features have been implemented into automobiles from most major manufacturers.

Advanced Driver Assistance Systems (ADAS) features

Advanced Driver Assistance Systems (ADAS) are a category of in-vehicle systems that help drivers improve safety and avoid collisions by providing warnings and implementing safeguards, and even – as a last resort – taking control of the vehicle to avoid a collision. While many ADAS features are made available by automobile manufacturers to boost selling points, some ADAS features may be recommended or even mandated by national safety authorities. For example, in the United States rear view cameras are mandated by the US National Highway Traffic Safety Administration (NHTSA) for vehicles sold after May 2018; while alcohol ignition interlock systems (which prevent the ignition from starting if alcohol is detected in the driver's breath) are recommended. A few conceptual examples of ADAS features are covered briefly in this section.

Collision avoidance

Collision warning systems process inputs from radar, laser and camera to identify the likelihood of a collision and provide warning cues such as vibration, warning lights and sound to make the driver aware of imminent danger. Collision avoidance also entails deeper actions such as autonomous application of brakes and/or control of steering. If you get too close to the vehicle in front of you, or do not brake fast enough when the vehicle in front of you slows down, your vehicle if equipped with a collision warning/avoidance system will issue warnings and even take control of your vehicle momentarily to apply brakes, in a timely manner. Computer system's reaction times can be better and more consistent than human reaction times. Human reaction times are obviously subject to variables such as emotions, moods, hormones, and headaches, and therefore expected to be less consistent compared to computing systems with adequate capabilities and sophistication.

Traffic sign recognition

Traffic sign recognition entails detecting the road signs such as stop signs, speed limits, and school zones, and warning the driver in case of imminent violations. These functions are accomplished by various technologies including computer vision and image processing and are covered in the next section.

Driver monitoring

Driver monitoring systems are based on sensors and technologies such as infrared LED, camera, eye tracking, that are used to infer the driver's lack of attentiveness or sleepiness; and to issue remedial warning sounds to help revive the driver's attention.

Vision enhancement

During times of poor visibility road conditions, enhanced vision systems can be useful in enhancing the user's perception and emphasizing poorly visible relevant entities such as obstacles, poorly visible vehicles, or road anomalies (during construction or acts of nature and environment, or otherwise). Such systems may use thermographic (infrared) camera technology to provide overlays in the windshield to enhance or emphasize visual information.

ADAS – supporting technologies

The synergistic combination of many diverse technologies – such as powerful processors, wireless connectivity, sensors for speed, vibration, light, radio waves, as well as cameras, imaging and computer vision, advanced software algorithms, and standards and protocols – serve to make ADAS a practical reality.

Super-computer in the vehicle

In recent years, the availability of increasingly powerful CPUs and graphical processing units (GPUs) in vehicular SoCs (System on a chip) have made real world implementation of ADAS features possible via real-time monitoring and processing of signals and data from the vehicle's internal systems, surrounding road and environmental conditions, as well as signals that represents the state of the driver. Advanced sensor technologies in conjunction with artificial intelligence and supercomputing capabilities serve as the foundation for more advanced ADAS features. Marvell, Qualcom, Texas Instruments, Freescale, and Nvidia are among the numerous SoC/processor manufacturers with offerings for the vehicular segment. In early 2016, Nvidia, the company well known for its GPU technology, announced its new Drive PX2 in-vehicle computing platform which it deemed as a supercomputer in the automobile.

Computer Vision

Computer vision pertains to the acquisition, processing, analysis and interpretation of image data. Autonomous cars leverage advanced algorithms and artificial intelligence to analyze sensor data to distinguish between real world objects, vehicles, lane markers, pedestrians, road signs, and traffic lights. Computer vision systems include image acquisition devices such as a camera/ sensor hardware, processors, and software to process the images and perform analysis and recognition. Many ADAS features depend on sophisticated computer vision algorithms.

LiDAR sensors

LiDAR (a blend of the words light and radar) is a surveying technology that can be used to measure the distance to surrounding objects and obstacles, by illuminating them with laser light and measuring the time it takes for the light to reflect back. Many vehicular technologies for obstacle detection and avoidance are based on LiDAR sensors.

Augmented Reality

Augmented reality pertains to complementation and enhancement of real world visual information, via overlays. Vision enhancement and object recognition are examples of augmented reality that is applied towards boosting the driver's perception beyond what is possible by the human eye alone. Some automobile manufacturers such as Chevrolet for example (http://www.chevrolet.com/culture/article/augmented-reality-technology.html) have developed windshields with augmented reality overlays that help enhance the visibility of poorly visible items of interest such as an unexpected pedestrian starting to cross the street, an erratically driving car, or a poorly visible curb.

Vehicle-to-Vehicle(V2V)

Vehicle-to-Vehicle(V2V) is a wireless peer-to-peer ad-hoc connectivity based technology that allows vehicles on the road to communicate live information – such as their presence on the road and current status such as speed, braking, direction, and failure/emergency – to other participating proximate vehicles. Information received via V2V can be made available to the driver as necessary, to complement human perception, and also be used to support co-ordination and collision avoidance functions. The primary goal of V2V is collision avoidance and safety.

Connectivity devices installed in vehicles use dedicated short range communications (DSRC), a short range communication technology that works up to a range of 300 meters and associated standards and protocols. In the United States, the Federal Communications Commission (FCC) has allocated 75MHz band of the 5.9 GHz spectrum for Intelligent Transportation Systems (ITS) communications. The European Telecommunications Standards Institute (ETSI) has allocated 30 MHz of the 5.9 GHz band for the purpose of vehicular communications. Many other nations such as Japan and Singapore have designated communication channels allocated by their respective regulatory authorities. IEEE 801.11p is an enhancement to the popular IEEE 802.11 Wi-Fi standard, that adds support for wireless access in vehicular environment and is pertinent to vehicular communication systems in the licensed Intelligent Transportation Systems (ITS) band.

The Car-2-Car Communication Consortium is an European industry organization – whose members include many major automobile and electronic hardware manufacturers worldwide – with the aim of developing an open set of standards for vehicle-to-vehicle communication across automobile models and manufacturers (as well as vehicle-to-infrastructure communication, which is covered in the following section). V2V thus makes it possible for vehicles to directly exchange collaborative and relevant information, within the operating range of about 300 meters – which is better than the range achievable via technologies that leverage camera, radar, or ultrasonic sensors.

Vehicle-to-Infrastructure(V2I)

Vehicle -to- Infrastructure (V2I) pertains to the communication between vehicles and their surrounding relevant infrastructural entities such as sections of roads, bridges, ramps, tollgates and parking areas. V2I communication can support many diverse use cases including dynamic speed management which can be useful during periods of high density of vehicles in a section of ramp, notification of the icy state of a section of bridge, or information about the location of parking spots. V2I technologies are thus aimed at road safety, as well as a convenience. V2I and V2V are both part of the vehicular ad-hoc network.

Autonomous car

Manual conventional driving is governed by a set of rules and process, and the act of manual driving is much like an algorithm under execution. The autonomous car – also known as the self-driving car – is a vehicle that can drive itself independently, without human control over its navigation and safety functions. The autonomous car senses its environment including road signs, traffic signals, pedestrians, other vehicles, and unexpected obstacles, and navigates to its – human designated – destination. Although autonomous cars appeared in the 1980s in academic and industry research environments, it has only been in recent years that the overall conditions have become conducive for this technology to arrive to the mass market. Today, autonomous cars are under active development for the mass market by many corporations, and use the same fundamental technologies that ADAS systems might use (such as LiDAR, radar, computer vision, motion sensors, and GPS), but operate at a far higher degree and scale in terms of computational algorithms and sensor inputs. Tesla, BMW, Google, Ford, Mercedes-Benz, Nissan, Toyota, Renault, Audi, Daimler, Kia, Baidu, AKKA Technologies, and GM, are some of the companies reportedly working on bringing autonomous cars and/or cars with advanced driver assistance features to the mass market in the near future.

The US National Highway Traffic Safety Administration (NHTSA) has proposed a formal classification system for autonomous cars with five levels that correspond to various degrees of automated and autonomous driving function. The basic level Level-0, entails all functions performed by the human driver. Level-1 pertains to individual automated controls such as automatic braking that the vehicle is capable of performing. Level-2 pertains to a multitude of automated controls that the vehicle is capable of performing, such as adaptive cruise control and lane centering. Level-3 pertains to vehicles that allow the driver to cede complete control to the vehicle's autonomous driving system under certain conditions. Level-4 pertains to vehicles that perform all driving functions on from start to finish for an entire trip, such that the human driver is not expected to take control of the car at any time. Level-4 classification corresponds to the technology that Google is reportedly working on developing. Google's self driving car model has had much coverage in the news in recent years. The car has a multitude of sensors, radars, and cameras mounted at various locations, the most prominent of which is the round sensor bank mounted on the roof of the car, in order to detect signals from all directions. The car's computational system processes the sensor inputs to create a 3-dimensional model of the surroundings including roads, lanes, obstructions, other vehicles, and pedestrians. The car's computational system is "aware" of it's current location down to its precise position within the lane on the road.

Consumer, social and market trends

In order for something that is technologically possible to actually reach the mass consumer market many diverse criteria often need to be met – such as monetary cost and social factors, as well as acceptable changes to existing human habits, usage patterns, and expectations. Interestingly, there have been many developments in recent years in the arena of consumer transportation and IoT style connected devices, appliances and equipment.

Car ride, sharing platforms

Car renting and sharing is a trend that has been emerging in recent years. Zipcar (now a subsidiary of Avis Budget Group) is an example of a hugely successful car sharing company that allows a consumer to rent and use a car by the hour or the day. Consumers pay a one time application fee and a small monthly membership fee before they are able to rent and Zipcars that are available in their vicinity. Zipcar members can use an access card or Zipcar's mobile phone (Android or iOS) app in order to unlock and drive the car that they have reserved for their trip. Zip car maintains its fleet of cars and each car has a parking location assigned to it, typically in some metro downtown area or an airport. Each vehicle needs to be returned at the end of the trip reservation to its assigned parking location. Zipcars use embedded radio-frequency identification transponders that communicate with the access car and mobile apps, in order to perform car access – locking and unlocking –

functions. Zipcars are currently available at particular metro areas and airports in particular countries in North America and Europe.

Getaround is a car sharing platform which uses a consumer peer-to-peer sharing model that allows their member car owners to rent out their own car to other members, during the periods that they are not using it themselves. Members who are needing cars are able to find cars for their trips, while the car owner members earn a set percentage of the rental revenue from renting out their cars. Individual car owners maintain their own vehicles and set the rental price, while Getaround the company organizes the auto insurance during the active rental period. Getaround does not maintain any fleet of vehicles.

Turo (formerly RelayRides) is another peer-to-peer car sharing platform that is similar to Getaround in that the company provides the platform that enables car owners and renters to connect. There are several other car sharing platforms worldwide, such as Stadtmobile, car2go, GoCar, Momo, Modo, MylesCar and YourDrive.

In the ride sharing model, consumers are able to pick the right car for the trip on hand, such as a small compact car to drive to downtown, as that may be advantageous in congested traffic conditions and scarce parking scenarios; or a larger sized vehicle for a weekend trip with the family. Ride sharing can make it more affordable for more consumers to enjoy the ride in a luxurious car of their choice, as prices will tend to vary by the time of the day and season, in a dynamic market place.

Uber and Lyft are two similar, popular, unconventional taxi platforms that allow consumers to submit trip requests via mobile phone based apps, which can be fulfilled by the respective platform drivers who work as independent contractors. While Uber operates worldwide in over 50 countries, Lyft reportedly operates within the US. Drivers gain access to flexible, independent jobs while consumers gain access to the choice of alternatives to conventional, regulated (and often overly regulated) taxis. With abundant availability of ride service providers, consumers are able to avoid car ownership and even driving themselves altogether. In many urban areas, parking spaces are in short supply and residents prefer to avoid car ownership.

In many urban metro areas such as the city of San Francisco, conventional taxis have perpetually been in short supply since a long time. Conventional taxis that are registered in the San Francisco Bay area – that includes cities neighboring the city of San Francisco – are regulated with regard to where they are allowed to pick up a fare, depending on the city that they are registered with. For instance, a conventional taxi registered in the city of Palo Alto (about 30 miles away) that drops off a passenger in the city of San Francisco is not allowed to pick up a local passenger with a destination within the city of San Francisco, as it is not licensed to operate there. Every day, many conventional taxi drivers who violate this San Francisco city rule are fined for this violation – or at least, this is what many a Bay area taxi driver has told me, first hand. It certainly appeared that the local city authorities in the Bay area do not practical inter-city taxi registration, portability and inter-operating agreements – in contrast to the many bilateral and multilateral trade agreements that are in place between nations from across the world. The rise of Uber and Lyft in the San Francisco Bay area as their initial market, stemmed partly from a fundamental lack of adequate and readily accessible conventional taxi transportation in the area. In many parts of the world, the rules and regulations pertaining to taxis have undergone very little change in half a century or longer. At the same time, there is certainly need for some checks and balances with regard to the regulation and deregulation of taxis and consumer transportation.

The new car sharing model fundamentally disassociates car usage from car ownership and allows consumers to choose the right car for the right occasion and trip, be it work, social or vacation. The model of unconventional taxis provides consumers with convenient access to rides in a free and open market. The lines that separate a taxi, from a shared car, and from a personal automobile have commenced to get blurry, in light of these recent trends.

Lower car ownership

There appears to be, among the millennial generation (also known as generation Y) – a demographic with birth years in the 1980s and 1990s or so – a preference for an urban (rather than a sub-urban) lifestyle. The vehicle as a personal financial asset depreciates rapidly and can incur unexpected maintenance costs. There is a trend towards reduced car ownership via car sharing, and walking, biking, and use of public transport.

IoT appliances, self ordering

IoT style connected household appliances are now commencing to exhibit the ability to self- order refills and spares when they are running low, if desired by the consumer. In early 2016, Amazon introduced its Dash Replenishment Service (DRS) which enables connected household devices and appliances to order spares autonomously once setup by the consumer. Brother, Samsung and other brands of printers are able to trigger placing orders for refill ink cartridges on Amazon, while washing machines may be able to trigger ordering detergent supplies. Such use cases become inevitable as devices, equipment and appliances with embedded computing devices and sensors are able to detect their internal state and needs, and take action as configured by the consumer/owner. In the case of the automobile, the detection of the need for maintenance and integration with the auto servicing locations, appointments and calendars and parts will be appreciated by many consumers.

Google Maps and ride services

In March 2016, Google announced that its Google Maps application will include an additional option of "Ride services", besides the existing standard options of driving, biking, walking, and public transportation. The new ride services option is expected to initially include ride services providers such as Uber, mytaxi in Germany and Spain, Hailo in the UK and Spain, 99Taxis in Brazil, Ola Cabs in India, Gett in the UK. Previously, consumers would have needed to use various apps for finding various ride services offering; while Google Maps will now provide a consolidated view of a multitude of ride service options alongside the standard options (such as public transport, car, biking, walking) thus making it more convenient for users. This addition to Google Maps indicates to me, the increasingly relevance of ride services. Depending on the trip and the timing, consumers may choose to drive themselves if they are in the mood, or opt for getting a ride if they are feeling a little under the weather or prefer to engage in other activities such as relaxing or napping.

Civic, safety and environmental factors

The need for a better way in the realm of personal transportation is universally recognized today by individual, community and government alike. Traffic congestion, increasing commute times, road accidents, parking problems, and overall driving related stress have become the norm worldwide.

Parking

Finding a parking spot is a big challenge in many urban metro areas. Numerous studies have shown that a significant percentage of traffic in many a downtown area represents drivers who are circling the block in search of a parking spot. Moreover, parking spaces take up a significant portion of prime real estate in many urban metros. This tends to drive up the per square foot cost of land, and reduce the availability of urban green spaces and parks for the community. Parking is prohibitively expensive in many metro areas. Most personal, non commercial vehicles end up remaining in a parked state for the most part – over 95% – of in their usage life span.

Safety

While on a long trip driving over the Raton pass in the high mountains near the New Mexico – Colorado border, in the spring of 2005, I encountered an unexpected snow storm. Several vehicles stopped and then hesitantly commenced to move slowly and tentatively under low visibility, heavy snow conditions. Interestingly, the various automobiles commenced to proceed in a single lane, uniformly and optimally spaced, coherent formation. The vehicle in front paved the way with some sense of support from the drivers behind in case of problems, while the ones behind had some semblance of assurance of drive-ability and safety based on the ones ahead. The vehicles behind appeared to monitor the safety of the ones in front, in tacit understanding. Depending on the increasing or decreasing intensity of the storm, the speed of this ad-hoc motorcade like formation adjusted gracefully and in unison. After several hours of such driving, the storm slowly cleared up and the vehicles commenced to pickup speed gradually and at some point the formation started to disband with the honking of horns and the waving of hands, in celebration of making it safely through this intense, unexpected snow storm. I learned that when danger is more apparent, our driving behavior is clearly capable of adequately factoring in the needs and concerns of safety, survival, and the driving community. Under more normal conditions however, it is less common to find coherent traffic that maintains safe braking distances and moves in a coherent, co-ordinated, and graceful manner. Road safety in typical rush hour traffic in many urban areas can be said to lie at the mercy of the worst or most careless or distracted drivers.

Insurance & technology

In the United States, automobile insurance is designed to cover the financial liability and loss of vehicle that the vehicle owner may face if their vehicle is involved in a collision resulting in property or physical damage. Vehicle owners typically pay insurance companies a monthly fee or insurance premium. Many states require vehicle owners to carry some minimum level of liability insurance. While driving licenses and insurance are governed by state laws, interstate driving is supported via Article IV, Section 2, Clause 1 or the Comity clause of the US Constitution which prohibits one US state from treating citizens of other states in a discriminatory manner.

According to the US department of transportation, there has been a general declining trend in vehicle crash fatalities on US roadways since year 2006 with minor exceptions. In 2014, the number of vehicle related fatalities stood at over 32,000 per year, while over 2.3 million individuals were estimated to be injured. In fact the number of crashes increased between 2013 and 2014, with about 8 percent of the crashes having no associated injuries, but with property damage. It is likely that improved safety features such as better airbags, serve to reduce human injuries when vehicle crashes occur. There have been an increase in alcohol related accidents per recent statistics. All 50 states in the United States have laws that permit the imposition of ignition interlock devices as a possible sentencing for drunken drivers. The ignition interlock device also known as the breath alcohol interlock requires the driver to blow into a mouthpiece prior to attempting to start their vehicle's ignition. If the breath sample fails, the vehicle will not start.

Insurance telematics

Auto insurance telematics entails monitoring and making driver behavior and statistics available to the insurance company at all times via installed sensors and/or access to the in-vehicle computer. The premiums vary based on the driver behavior and driving patterns – reducing if the quality of driving is less risky, and visa versa. Smartphone apps based telematics too can serve this same purpose. Insurance telematics is a growing segment that can benefit the consumer as the usage based insurance model can result in reduced premiums based on the individual driver's specifics of their driving (rather than mass statistics).

Environment and resource conservation

Historically, the United States has been on the forefront of the individual car ownership model of transportation and also the largest market for cars worldwide. Today, we are seeing the rise of the new economies of many regions of the world such as Asia, South America, Eastern Europe and Africa. With the growth of human population and a correspondingly increasing number of automobiles manufactured, the environmental impact from the current model of automobile transportation will tend to increase significantly and become less sustainable.

Automobile transportation revolution

While new technology can progress rapidly, ingrained human habits and expectations tend to evolve relatively slowly. After a lifetime of getting accustomed to driving "oneself" in one's "own" car, it can be difficult to imagine something radically different. Yet, there have been progressive and incremental changes in vehicles such that drivers have begun to get accustomed to many of the ADAS features such as crash avoidance braking and lane violation warnings. There is already a pay-per-ride model of consumer transportation that represents a small segment of the market share. Today, a coincidence of many factors have resulted in the likelihood of a new revolution in automobile transportation. Typically consumers have been buying an automobile that they retain for several years. In practice, the same car may not serve as the ideal vehicle for widely divergent needs during the week, season, and year – for example, the daily commute, the weekend trip, or a long road trip in summer. Cars tend to depreciate in market value immediately after purchase. Therefore, it is not cost effective to buy a new car and trade in an used car often.

There can be advantages for everyone if transportation is modeled as a service that dissociates car usage from car ownership. This is a major change though as historically there has been a tight coupling between usage and ownership. Today the pace of innovation in automobiles is quite rapid, and this can motivate automobile enthusiasts to yearn for the latest model every year. But the car is a significantly bigger investment compared to the cell phone. As a service, cars can become more accessible to more consumers.

Per ride basis, automobile service, ride provider

The per ride basis of transportation is currently on the rise, due to the Uber and Lyft model of transportation. This model de-emphasizes individual car ownership. Reduced car ownership and the rise in per ride basis of individual transportation creates room for the self driving/ autonomous car. The consumer will likely be able to choose between a human driven car or an autonomous one.

While autonomous cars are expected to be available for individual ownership, they are also well suited for the per ride based model of transportation as a service. Autonomous cars are likely to be expensive initially, so it is likely that they will fit in better with the per ride based transportation as a service model. Ride providers will likely find it worthwhile to acquire and maintain a fleet of autonomous cars in particular markets. At some point in the not so distant future, self driving cars will arrive to the location, at the time that they are needed by passengers – judging by the pace of progress of technology in this arena.

If a ride in a high end car is made more affordable for a large number of consumers in a dynamically priced market, a new market segment is created and the car sharing platform owners have a potential revenue stream that is dependent on car rides, rather than a car sale. A given consumer may purchase a new car say every 6 years on average, but they may avail of several car rides a day from one or more car ride provider. Thus, by participating in the development of car sharing platforms and its new economy, the new model of revenue stream is associated with the "consumer trip/ride basis" rather than the "consumer car purchase basis".

By engaging with the millions of consumer car rides per day in the new shared and intelligent automobile economy in a dynamic pricing model, ride platform owners and automakers who are invested or engaged in this economy have great potential for significant revenue and profitability. This is an ecosystem that can make it exciting both for consumers and for the auto industry service providers. In the transportation as a service model, a far fewer number of cars can adequately meet consumer's transport needs; and less congestion around parking spaces is likely due to greater flexibility regarding parking.

Impact of reduced car ownership

The reduction in the world wide demand for automobile purchases – due to the trend of reduced automobile ownership and sharing, may seem at first to be bad news for auto-makers. The cost of each intelligent and/or autonomous car will surely go up and manufacturing volumes will tend to down and yet many other relevant parameters can open new opportunities and boost the potential for greater profitability. Many automakers are already participating in the new economic model of automobile rides and self driving cars. General Motors for instance is a major investor in Lyft. Daimler, BMW and other major automobile makers have commenced building their own pay per ride based transportation services. Fundamentally, manufacturing volume and profitability are not co-incident in many industries including the auto-industry. Many high volume manufacturing based market segments tend to be slave to low profit margins and fluctuating consumer demand. Today, traditional auto-makers are innovating and rethinking the automobile experience and even racing towards building self driving cars and/or participating in the car sharing platforms.

Legal considerations, autonomous cars

There are indications that the US governmental regulatory bodies including the NHTSA aim to recognize computer and artificial intelligence based "drivers", thus paving the way for autonomous cars to become a reality in the consumer market place. With regard to automobile accidents, human witness and observations tend to be subjective. Modern cars on the other hand have event data recorders which record various sensor data that can be used to determine matters more objectively. In case of autonomous vehicles, sensor, camera, V2V and V2I communication data primarily serve to avoid collisions and improve safety, however the recorded and logged data can serve to pinpoint the cause of accidents more objectively and also support refinement and improvement of the safety algorithms. With adequate refinements to the legal framework in the long run, the data recorded in vehicles may be able to help determine the cause of accidents in a more objective and deterministic matter.

Privacy considerations, connected cars

Much like the widespread use of smart phones (apps, location tracking, and sensors) raises issues of consumer data privacy, the use of connected "smart" vehicles brings attention to the matter of consumer and vehicular data privacy. The growing use of IoT devices including the connected automobile typically entails an every growing mass of consumer device data that may be collected and retained on the cloud – it raises growing concerns for consumer rights, data breach and misuse, and transparency and control over such data. If consumers have awareness of what data is collected and by who and for what purpose, and have control over the use, sharing and deletion of the data, that makes for better consumer privacy. Data anonymization and encryption during transmission and storage are important and align with good data privacy. Cloud service providers and device makers who publish their data collection, transmission, and storage policies to make them transparent and easy for consumers to understand are better aligned with good data privacy.

Figure 9-2 shows the *Android Auto* App's permissions which allows users to exercise fine grained control over various permissions, on devices running Android 6/Marshmallow and onward. This is an example of a desirable privacy model that gives consumers control over individual nuggets of data and is easy to understand and use.

With regard to consumer data storage on the cloud, Google for example allows you view your own history data, export or "takeout" all your Google data (including location and map history, *Google Fit* data, email, photo, videos, documents, emails, etc.), also delete your Google account altogether. These functions makes it possible for you have visibility into the collected data, use your own data per your own needs, import your data (that you have export out of Google) into another service of your choice. Google publishes their data security policies from end to end: https://cloud.google.com/security. With regard to security in the Android device, more information can be found at : https://source.android.com/security/.

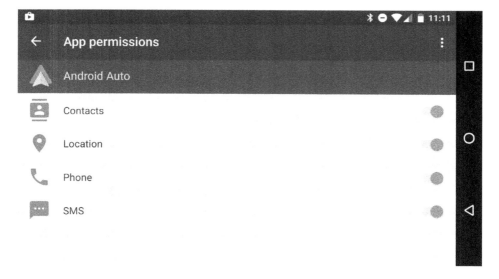

Figure **9-2** User control over Android Auto via permissions

The NHTSA for example envisages machine to machine PKI (public key infrastructure) for encryption of data exchanged in V2I interactions in order to ensure data privacy and security. More information is available at:

http://www.safercar.gov/staticfiles/safercar/v2v/V2V_Fact_Sheet_101414_v2a.pdf and
http://www.nhtsa.gov/staticfiles/rulemaking/pdf/V2V/V2V-ANPRM_081514.pdf

Safety, connected cars

As we covered earlier in this book, *Android Auto* apps are required to be digitally signed and released via the Google Play store, before they can be executed on a real automobile head-unit. Google as the platform owner thus insists that the app code is digitally signed, the app publisher is authenticated, and has accepted the *Android Auto Addendum*. Apps undergo a manual review processes before the app code can be executed in the runtime environment in the head-unit. These are some of the steps that boost safety and data privacy in the *Android Auto* connected car.

In the arena of the core automobile technology, there is on the one hand the matter of safety and effectiveness of new ADAS and autonomous driving technologies under diverse real world scenarios; and it will need some time before adequate statistics that give us deeper perspective in this regard become available. The connected car also brings up matters of the potential for car hacking or hijacking which entails the electronic unauthorized access to the vehicle's functions. Vehicle manufacturers typically use engineering practices that emphasize isolation and segregation of the infotainment computing and wiring circuits from the core automobile computing and wiring. Vehicle manufacturers have reportedly been working on hardening the technology stack to prevent unauthorized access in their connected cars.

In-vehicle infotainment in the future

In the near future, we are likely to see some of the incremental expansions of *Android Auto* into new arenas covered earlier in this chapter. In the long run, as and when autonomous cars become available in the not too distant future, the nature of in-vehicle infotainment will change dramatically. As a passenger in an autonomous car, your in-vehicle infotainment system will not need to be restrictive as is the case today – you will be able to enjoy your favorite movies or games during on your ride. You might even be able to get some office or school work or book reading done while on your car ride!

Thanks for reading !

Please visit http://androidautobook.info/ for source code and errata.

References and further reading

https://en.wikipedia.org/wiki/Peak_car
http://inventors.about.com/library/weekly/aacarsassemblya.htm
https://developers.google.com/android/reference/com/google/android/gms/package-summary
http://developer.android.com/guide/components/aidl.html
https://en.wikipedia.org/wiki/Drive_by_wire
https://en.wikipedia.org/wiki/Carburetor
https://en.wikipedia.org/wiki/Traffic_sign_recognition
https://en.wikipedia.org/wiki/Advanced_driver_assistance_systems
https://en.wikipedia.org/wiki/Collision_avoidance_system
https://en.wikipedia.org/wiki/Automotive_night_vision
https://en.wikipedia.org/wiki/Emergency_brake_assist
https://en.wikipedia.org/wiki/Radar
https://en.wikipedia.org/wiki/Lidar
http://www.nvidia.com/content/tegra/automotive/pdf/autonomous-cars-no-longer-just-science-fiction.pdf
http://nvidianews.nvidia.com/news/nvidia-boosts-iq-of-self-driving-cars-with-world-s-first-in-car-artificial-intelligence-supercomputer
http://www.detroitnews.com/story/business/autos/2016/01/05/nvidia-creates-first-automotive-supercomputer/78335558/
http://www.engadget.com/2016/01/04/nvidia-drive-px2/
http://techcrunch.com/2016/01/04/nvidia-announces-new-drive-px-2-supercomputer-in-a-lunchbox-for-self-driving-cars/
https://en.wikipedia.org/wiki/Graphics_processing_unit
http://www.chevrolet.com/culture/article/augmented-reality-technology.html
https://en.wikipedia.org/wiki/Millennials
https://en.wikipedia.org/wiki/Vehicle-to-vehicle
https://en.wikipedia.org/wiki/Vehicular_ad_hoc_network
https://en.wikipedia.org/wiki/ZMP_INC.
https://en.wikipedia.org/wiki/Driver_Monitoring_System
https://en.wikipedia.org/wiki/Telematics#Auto_insurance
http://www.safercar.gov/
http://www.safercar.gov/staticfiles/safercar/v2v/V2V_Fact_Sheet_101414_v2a.pdf
http://www-nrd.nhtsa.dot.gov/Pubs/812246.pdf
https://www.car-2-car.org
http://www.placemakers.com/2012/04/09/generation-ys-great-migration/
http://techcrunch.com/2014/12/16/american-re-urbanization-drives-more-on-demand-innovation/
http://www.pcmag.com/article2/0,2817,2498102,00.asp
https://www.amazon.com/oc/dash-replenishment-service
http://www.its.dot.gov/factsheets/v2isafety_factsheet.htm
http://ieeecss.org/sites/ieeecss.org/files/documents/IoCT-Part4-13VehicleToVehicle-HR.pdf
https://en.wikipedia.org/wiki/On-board_diagnostics

https://en.wikipedia.org/wiki/Graphics_processing_unit

http://www.bbc.com/news/technology-35235316

http://www.eetimes.com/author.asp?section_id=36&doc_id=1328609

https://developers.google.com/maps/documentation/android-api/

https://www.google.com/selfdrivingcar/

https://www.google.com/selfdrivingcar/how/

https://www.google.com/selfdrivingcar/faq/

http://www.engadget.com/2016/01/09/googles-self-driving-cars-dont-crash-as-much-as-humans-do/

https://maps.googleblog.com/2016/03/your-car-has-arrived-more-ways-to-get.html

https://en.wikipedia.org/wiki/United_States_Constitution

https://en.wikipedia.org/wiki/Google_Takeout

https://takeout.google.com/settings/takeout

https://en.wikipedia.org/wiki/Google_Data_Liberation_Front

https://en.wikipedia.org/wiki/Lyft

https://en.wikipedia.org/wiki/CAN_bus

http://www.marketwatch.com/story/self-driving-cars-will-kill-the-auto-industry-2016-01-06

https://en.wikipedia.org/wiki/Carsharing

https://en.wikipedia.org/wiki/Getaround

http://www.motherjones.com/environment/2016/01/future-parking-self-driving-cars

http://www.nytimes.com/2016/01/15/business/us-proposes-spending-4-billion-on-self-driving-cars.html

http://www.wsj.com/articles/regulators-willing-to-consider-computer-driven-car-1455117797

http://inventors.about.com/library/weekly/aacarsassemblya.htm

http://www.its.dot.gov/factsheets/v2isafety_factsheet.htm#sthash.ghs5eFHA.dpuf

http://www.its.dot.gov/factsheets/v2isafety_factsheet.htm

https://en.wikipedia.org/wiki/Vehicular_communication_systems

https://en.wikipedia.org/wiki/CAN_bus

https://en.wikipedia.org/wiki/Event_data_recorder

http://www.scientificamerican.com/article/why-car-hacking-is-nearly-impossible/

http://www.gartner.com/smarterwithgartner/staying-on-track-with-connected-car-security/

https://en.wikipedia.org/wiki/Data_anonymization

https://fpf.org/issues/connected-cars/

https://en.wikipedia.org/wiki/Public_key_infrastructure

http://www.nhtsa.gov/staticfiles/rulemaking/pdf/V2V/V2V-ANPRM_081514.pdf

http://www.safercar.gov/staticfiles/safercar/v2v/V2V_Fact_Sheet_101414_v2a.pdf

Index

Symbols

www.ingramcontent.com/pod-product-compliance
Lightning Source LLC
Chambersburg PA
CBHW080408060326

40689CB00019B/4169

* 9 7 8 1 5 1 8 6 7 2 4 6 0 *